SHINING THROUGH

Finding the balance between heartache and hope while raising a child with special needs

LIANA CANCIAN

Copyright © 2024 by Liana Cancian

All rights reserved.

Published and Distributed in Canada by Live Life Happy Publishing.
www.livelifehappypublishing.com

All rights reserved. No part of this book may be reproduced by any mechanical, photographic, or electronic process, or in the form of a phonograph recording: Nor may it be stored in a retrieval system, transmitted, or otherwise be copied for public or private use- other than for "fair use" as brief quotations embodied in articles and reviews without prior written permission of the publisher. If you use any of the information in this book for yourself, which is your constitutional right, the author and the publisher assumes no responsibility for your actions.

Library of Congress Cataloging-in-Publication Data

Liana Cancian

Shining Through

Categories:

Parenting & Relationships> Self-Help & Personal Transformation > Special Needs Parenting

ISBN Paperback: 978-1-990461-74-3

ISBN E-Book: 978-1-990461-74-3

Cover Design: Live Life Happy Publishing

Live Life Happy Publishing

PUBLISHER'S NOTE & AUTHOR DISCLAIMER

This publication is designed to provide accurate and authoritative information concerning the subject matter covered. It is sold to understand that the publisher and author are not engaging in or rendering any psychological, medical or other professional services. If expert assistance or counselling is needed, seek the services of a competent medical professional. For immediate support call your local crisis line. The following book could contain actual events and experiences that the author has encountered in their life. However, some names and specific locations have been changed or omitted to protect the privacy and confidentiality of the individuals involved. The changes do not alter the story's integrity or its messages.

Dedicated to Olivia,

Though you may never read the words on these pages in this lifetime, may your journey serve as a beacon of hope, inspiring countless souls to persevere and never lose sight of hope.

I dedicate this book to everyone who has taken part in Olivia's earthly journey. You know who you are!

Contents

Destined Connection 12
Blessed Beginnings 18
In The Shadow Of Blessings 22
Torn Between Fear And Faith 26
Feeling Suckerpunched 28
The Calm Before The Storm 30
Unravelling The Uncontrollable: Facing The Diagnosis 32
Redefining Resilience 36
Behind The Mask Of Dignity 39
Beyond The Prescription 41
A Beacon In The Darkness 43
Juggling Grief And Gratitude 47
A Time To Heal 51
Surgical Crossroads 55
Putting Trust In Science 60
Glorious Awakening 62
In The Hands Of Hope 64
Heart In Hand 67
A Fresh Start 73
Bittersweet Homecoming 75
Shattered Hopes 78
Embracing The Lifeline 80
Finding Solace In Nature 82
God Must Hate You 85

Expanding Our Hearts 88
My Sister's Keeper 96
Seize The Opportunity 101
The Unexpected Detour 104
Courage In The Face Of Change 107
New Year, New Home, New Hope 112
Empowered By Unity Through Thick And Thin 116
Unexpected Blessings 120
From Struggle To Superpower 123
Our Ray Of Sunshine 126
The Bumpy Road To Ketosis 129
Angels In Scrubs 134
Heavenly Helpers 137
Surviving Not Thriving 143
Deciding Her Destiny 147
Grief Knows No Boundaries 153
Reinventing Yourself 155
Beyond The Pages 172
Heartfelt Tribute 174

NURTURED BY LOVE

My journey began in the late 1970s as part of a close-knit Italian immigrant family. Stepping into a world rooted in tradition and love, I was immediately embraced by the warmth that defined our quintessential upbringing. While my father worked tirelessly at an automotive factory, my mother poured her heart and soul into being a devoted stay-at-home mom. Our humble abode may not have boasted extravagant luxuries, but it was rich in something far more valuable and irreplaceable- *love.*

Within the modest walls of our home, my mother reigned as the resilient matriarch, ensuring a structured and disciplined environment, while my father's unwavering work ethic sustained us through his laborious shifts. Their dedication to our family's well-being was evident in every sacrifice they made. Each of them had a distinct role, and their harmonious partnership was a powerful example. The values of determination and respect were instilled in us from an early age as we witnessed their dedicated support for one another. Our family thrived within clear boundaries, and I held a deep respect for them, fearing the loss of their respect in return. Compassion, self-love, and treating others with dignity were the bedrock of our family's core values.

My childhood was uniquely shaped as the youngest among two considerably older brothers. Our dinner table was a space for profound conversations beyond my years. We engaged in thought-provoking discussions about various topics, from current events to philosophical ideas. These mealtime conversations created a sense of connection and intimacy within our family. They nourished not only our bodies but also our minds and souls.

Those discussions became invaluable sources of wisdom and knowledge, shaping my understanding of the world and influencing the person I embody today. I hold those memories close to my heart, grateful for the upbringing that fostered maturity and a deep engagement with the world.

I consider myself incredibly fortunate to have received unwavering support from my parents throughout my upbringing. They modelled an immense sense of determination and a strong work ethic, which I absorbed through their example. Their consistent encouragement instilled in me the belief that I could overcome any challenge. They expressed their admiration for me daily, reminding me how blessed they felt to have **ME** as their child. Their love and affection guided me through my formative years, ensuring I always felt profoundly cherished and valued, regardless of my mistakes.

I am eternally grateful for the profound influence my upbringing has had on shaping my identity. It has sparked a relentless thirst for knowledge, a resilience to tackle obstacles, and a sincere desire to impact the world positively. Who I am today is a result of those collective experiences.

From an early age, I discovered a deep love for people, especially my friends. With no biological sisters, my closest friends formed my chosen sisterhood. Aligned in values and morals, we effortlessly supported each other on a righteous path. Trouble rarely found me; the mere notion of disappointing my parents churned my stomach.

Throughout my academic journey, teachers consistently commended me and my parents for my logical thinking and level-headedness. It was a quality that set me apart, and as a result, I was frequently selected to lead student-led groups that aimed to assist those in need. I always had a deep interest in and appreciation for individuals from diverse backgrounds, and I felt a profound sense of responsibility to care for and support them. I believe this nurturing trait is something I inherited from my mother, who has always been the epitome of compassion and always ready to lend a helping hand.

During my time in elementary school, my brother and I had the opportunity to volunteer and assist children with special needs. Although we didn't fully understand why we were chosen, our parents encouraged us to embrace the experience. The classrooms of these children were filled with vibrant and captivating elements, like jumbo bean bag chairs, colourful ladders, and an array of exhilarating toys, at least that's what it felt like from a child's perspective. Among these remarkable individuals was one special friend who instantly touched my heart—Little Elizabeth. She was my age at the time, and despite her developmental functions being that of a three-year-old, our connection was immediate and profound. Together, Elizabeth and I formed a unique bond. I took delight in teaching her how to read while she amazed me with her clever toy tricks. We shared countless moments of joy, including our special swimming outings outside of the school. Reflecting on those times, I realize I was learning as much from her as she was from me. Even at a young age, I was captivated by their unique qualities. In my eyes, she was magical. As though she was put on this earth for a reason that was yet to be determined.

While others may have overlooked or mocked her, I innately felt a powerful drive to defend and protect her as if guided by an unexplainable force. In these extraordinary individuals, I saw something far greater than their disabilities or abnormalities. Little did I know then that these early experiences laid the foundation for my future path. As I reflect on the past, I hold a strong belief that every event in life unfolds for a distinct reason. During those early experiences, a journey of higher purpose began to take shape. Deep within, I had an unwavering conviction that there was a grander plan in store for me, orchestrated by a divine force. God, the architect of my future, held the blueprint that laid out a path carefully crafted to enable me to create a profound and meaningful impact in the lives of others. Although I remained unaware of the intricate details within that blueprint, I held onto the faith that it would guide me toward my destined purpose.

Being an A-type personality, I possessed an innate need to plan out every aspect of my life meticulously. My trusty leather-bound agenda, which oftentimes I got ridiculed for, became my constant companion, housing my carefully crafted plans and backup alternatives in case things didn't go as expected. This level of preparedness was both a blessing and a curse, and only time would reveal which side held.

One thing was crystal clear: I was determined to achieve greatness and make my parents proud by becoming the first university graduate in our family. With a razor focus, I embarked on my educational journey at the University of Toronto, which was a mere 15-minute commute from home and having the presence of my closest friends enrolled in the same program, fueled my confidence. I was convinced I had everything perfectly figured out, and it felt like the world was at my fingertips. I felt invincible! I had everything I needed and wanted, and life was good. Really good!

One of our very first family photo in 1980. Nico (9), Rocky (7), myself (2)

Celebrating our parents 25th Wedding Anniversary. From left to right: My oldest brother Nico(24), myself (16), my father, my mother, my brother Rocky (22)

DESTINED CONNECTION

One fateful evening in June 1998, I crossed paths with a young gentleman named Mark at a local bar called "Elbow Room" in my suburban town of Mississauga, just outside of Toronto. Little did I know that this seemingly ordinary encounter would begin a life-changing journey. From the moment we started talking, I was captivated by his genuine nature and compassionate spirit. Despite the recent loss of his brother, he exuded a raw authenticity that drew me in. It was clear that he carried a depth and maturity beyond his years, and I felt intrigued.

As our relationship blossomed, I gradually began to see the qualities that Mark saw in me. He envisioned a life filled with love, shared aspirations, and mutual growth, and he believed wholeheartedly that I was meant to be a part of it. At the time, I wasn't sure if I believed in his vision or shared the same level of certainty, but Mark's persistence and unwavering determination gradually won me over. I was head over heels! I fell deeply in love with him, drawn to his sincere nature and humble demeanor. Encountering someone genuine, free from personal agendas or concealed motives, was incredibly refreshing. Mark devoted himself entirely to our relationship, showcasing exceptional generosity, compassion, and selflessness – qualities that had guided me in my upbringing over the years. It felt familiar to me, and for that, I was all in.

I often wondered how fortunate I had been to find my perfect soulmate. Could it have been a personal manifestation over the years, or was it maybe a higher power at work, with Mark's late brother Allan playing a part in aligning us together? Regardless of the reason, we embarked on a journey together, bound by love and a shared vision of the future. Little did I know that this voyage would profoundly shape our lives and create an unbreakable bond that would withstand the tests of time.

After our initial encounters, Mark was eager for me to meet his family, whom he held in high regard. I could feel his genuine love and admiration for them in the words he spoke and how he carried himself, which was truly a breath of fresh air. His depth extended far beyond his often sombre expression, revealing a complexity that captivated me and drew me in. Despite his challenges, he constantly reassured me of his happiness, even if his facial expressions seldom mirrored it. I could sense the heaviness of heartbreak and sorrow he carried after his recent loss. My nurturing instincts drove me to aid him in navigating this challenging period and bringing back joy into his life. It became my mission to help him through this difficult time, driven by the belief in his immense potential hidden beneath his pain-stricken eyes and melancholic demeanor.

With determination, I set out to explore the depths of his soul, offering unwavering understanding and support in every possible way. I knew that beyond his serious facade lay untapped strength waiting to be unleashed, and it became my heartfelt duty to guide him through the darkness and help him rediscover the light within.

This journey wasn't a fleeting gesture; it was a long-term commitment. I was prepared to dedicate myself wholeheartedly to witness his growth and flourishing again.

One sunny Saturday in July, we headed to Georgian Bay to visit Mark's parents on their beloved boat. It quickly became apparent that boating held a special place in their hearts, as it had played a significant role in their cherished childhood memories. They dedicated weekends to exploring the islands and creating precious moments with loved ones in tow. What struck me was their openness and acceptance of people from all backgrounds, as they treated everyone with love and respect and in turn, were equally loved and cherished. Witnessing their strong bond and the boat's significance in their lives illuminated the depth of Mark's appreciation for his family. The boat became a symbol of their shared memories and a place where they could come together to celebrate and honour those moments, especially in the wake of their son's passing.

Arriving at the marina in Midland, Ontario, we embarked on Mark's late brother's boat, a poignant reminder of his absence. It marked the initial occasion for Mark to take the helm since his brother's passing. In a moment of sombre reflection, he exuded a poised demeanour, seemingly recalling the profound significance the boat held for him. I observed him navigate the waves with effortless skill while his hair glistened in the sunshine. This boat ride was a symbolic gesture, expressing Mark's attempt to move forward and, perhaps, conveying our shared love in a silent tribute to his brother.

Approaching his parents' grand white Carver boat, I was struck by its impressive beauty, surpassing my expectations. The boat was filled with many people eagerly awaiting our arrival. Stepping onto their boat marked a significant milestone in our relationship, and I was excited to meet the individuals who had shaped Mark into the wonderful person he was. Mark's parents, sister, and friends instantly greeted me at the stern of the boat with warm smiles and genuine hospitality, radiating a comforting presence that made me feel at home.

Surprisingly, they were thrilled to meet me, and their happiness instantly eased my nerves. Throughout the day, we engaged in meaningful conversations and even shared a meal together. A memorial picture of Allan, their late son, graced the dining table, a reminder of their recent loss. Despite their sorrow, they showed remarkable strength and resilience as they navigated through their pain. It became clear why Mark had displayed such strength and composure despite the fresh wound of losing his brother. I couldn't fathom the pain he was experiencing and the ability to move on with such resilience. It was a testament to his inner strength.

As the day went on, I struggled to maintain my composure as the weight of the family's grief and the unfamiliar motion of the boat stirred a mix of emotions within me. While I cherished every moment spent with them wholeheartedly, my queasy stomach reminded me of my novice boating skills and the physical demands it brought. Nonetheless, this experience sparked a profound appreciation for the boating lifestyle, and it marked the beginning of our shared love and passion for boating.

As the sun began to set, I reluctantly bid farewell to Mark's parents and their boat. It was a day filled with a whirlwind of emotions. The encounter left me with a deep sense of gratitude for being embraced by such a loving family. Meeting them allowed me to gain insight into the nurturing environment that shaped Mark's character and I was so exhilarated for what was yet to come.

Four short years later, we stood at the altar, exchanging vows and embarking on our lifelong journey together. After the wedding celebrations, we decided to begin our married life in the charming town of Bolton, located 30 miles north of my childhood home. It was a significant adjustment for me, leaving behind the familiarity of my close-knit family and the small city of Mississauga, which I had called home for so long.

Yet, the priceless teachings of confidence and self-love, imprinted by my parents, have remained steadfast throughout my existence. Their unwavering support and belief in me helped me navigate this change, making it easier to adapt to new and unfamiliar environments.

In the initial stages of our marriage, we uprooted twice, driven by the quest for fresh opportunities and new adventures. Mark's eagerness for novel experiences and openness to change consistently influenced our path, marking the commencement of my acclimatization to life's ever-shifting dynamics

Despite my initial hesitance, rooted in a background of simplicity and tradition, I quickly learned the skill to adapt and fully embrace each new circumstance. This marked the beginning of my quest to master the art of adaptation, a skill that flourished and refined over time. Our family's best interests always steered our decisions, gradually building my trust and support for Mark's vision.

Amidst the discomfort and uncertainty often accompanying change, I recognized its integral role in our unfolding narrative. I gradually let go of my attachment to familiarity, embracing each new adventure with open arms. While not without challenges, having Mark by my side provided invaluable guidance and unwavering support. Together, we discovered reservoirs of strength that empowered us to navigate uncharted territories. In each other's presence, we felt unstoppable, ready to conquer any obstacle that crossed our path. As long as we were together, we felt we could take on the world, that we were unstoppable!

Our wedding day - Sept 21, 2002

BLESSED BEGINNINGS

During our second year of marriage, we happily welcomed the arrival of our firstborn child Julian Allan, a joyous and transformative milestone in our lives.

Becoming parents was a monumental shift that completely transformed our lives. The simplest tasks, like cooking or grocery shopping, suddenly required meticulous planning and coordination. The colic phase, which seemed to stretch on for an eternity, tested our patience and resilience to the core. But as the days turned into weeks and months, we witnessed a remarkable change in our little one. His gentle and peaceful nature began to shine through, bringing us an overwhelming sense of joy and awe. Seeing the world through his innocent eyes was truly magical, as every day became an adventure filled with new discoveries. Our dreams and aspirations for our future as a family unfolded before us, and we eagerly embraced every opportunity to create precious memories with our beloved Julian. Whether it was embarking on exciting trips to Florida or enjoying the serenity of boating on Georgian Bay, we were a powerful trio, the world was our oyster, and we couldn't wait to discover it together.

As the twelve-month mark approached, an important decision loomed over us—whether I should return to the workforce or continue staying at home. Although both of us were raised by stay-at-home mothers and recognized the value of it, the prospect of giving up my job as a pharmaceutical rep that I had worked so hard to obtain was a difficult pill to swallow. I wrestled with the idea of leaving my career behind, as I was not yet ready to make that move. At the same time, the thought of entrusting our precious baby to daycare didn't align with our desires for his upbringing. After extensive discussions and careful consideration, we decided it would be best for me to remain at home and not resume my career. It was one tough decision but a necessary one.

Choosing to be a stay-at-home parent, and fully dedicating myself to the care and upbringing of Julian was a challenging adjustment; however, it became my new role that I learned to embrace wholeheartedly over time. If I was going to do it, I had to be the best I could be at it and give it my all. That was how I operated! As time passed, I grew to appreciate the immense joy of being there for every one of Julian's milestones while striving to cultivate a warm and nurturing home environment, much like our mothers provided us.

Despite occasional stress, staying at home with Julian was the most gratifying and self-fulfilling experience. I held gratitude close to my heart, fully aware of the privilege it was. I acknowledged the challenges many mothers faced in balancing work and home life. It often struck me how fortunate I was to have the choice to prioritize being the best mom I could be, especially when many of my friends didn't have that option. Even when I considered returning to the workforce or pursuing activities outside the home, my duty as Julian's mother grounded me, and those thoughts quickly faded.

As time went on and Julian grew, I began partaking in many mom-and-baby classes and programs which filled most of my days. It allowed me to socialize with other mothers while cherishing the opportunity to be present for his formative years.

Feeling like we had parenting down pat with Julian, we found expanding our family quite attractive. So, we promptly decided to have another baby before the notion lost its lustre. Fortunately for us, conception happened as soon as we began trying.

Both of my pregnancies brought me immense joy and fulfillment. Throughout those magical nine months, I experienced a newfound vitality and a deep sense of purpose. I felt destined to be pregnant. It was as if my body thrived during this time, and I embraced every moment with gratitude. Each pregnancy made me feel radiant and empowered, knowing I was nurturing a precious life. Taking care of myself became a top priority, attending prenatal classes and engaging in yoga sessions to stay physically and mentally healthy. Connecting with other expectant mothers was a source of immense support and excitement as we shared in anticipation of motherhood. Each day was filled with wonder and a sense of anticipation for the incredible journey ahead. It was one of the happiest times of my life, and I enjoyed every minute of it.

One night, as I kissed little Julian on the forehead and tucked him into bed, my mind was overcome with excitement and anticipation for what the future held for our growing family. We were young, healthy, and filled with vitality and happiness. During those quiet moments, I often let my imagination run wild, envisioning my dreams and aspirations for all of us.

I would grab my little leather-bound agenda and jot down big and small dreams. It became a ritual for me, a way to capture those fleeting thoughts and aspirations. ***I believed in the power of intention and manifestation; writing them down felt like taking the first step toward turning those dreams into reality.***

With our hearts full of love and our minds brimming with hope, we eagerly anticipated the arrival of our second child. We were ready to embrace the joys and challenges of expanding our family, knowing that together, we could create a future filled with love, happiness, and endless possibilities.

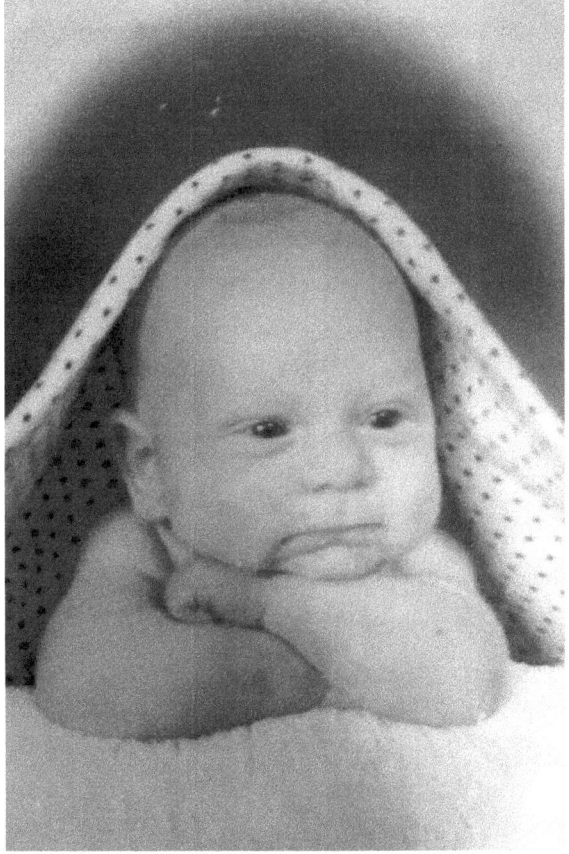

Julian at 3 weeks old

IN THE SHADOW OF BLESSINGS

It was midnight on May 24, 2006, when the long-awaited moment began. Exhausted and feeling uncomfortably bloated, I prepared myself for bed, unaware that the impending arrival of our second child was about to unfold. As I lay my head down, pondering whether the acupuncture sessions I had recently undergone or the prenatal yoga earlier in the day were responsible for the sudden discomfort, my body finally made its declaration. After 41 long weeks, my water decided to break, as if the baby was determined to make its big splash into the world. The time had finally come, and there was no turning back.

My husband Mark and I couldn't help but chuckle as we pondered why our babies seemed to have impeccable timing, choosing the most inconvenient moments to make their grand entrance. "Wouldn't it be nice if they could wait until after a good night's sleep?" we jokingly remarked. But deep down, we knew that life rarely goes according to plan, and we were excited and ready, despite our fatigue, to embrace the arrival of our new addition. It had been a week past the due date, and the anticipation had peaked. Our little ones had grown accustomed to the snug comfort of my womb, but it was time for them to enter our family and embrace the world awaiting them. Filled with confidence and preparedness, we ascended into our truck which was packed and loaded with all the necessary hospital gear way in advance. I was grateful for my organized nature which undoubtedly came in handy, especially at this critical moment. With the contractions intensifying and growing closer together, Mark seized the opportunity to navigate the roads with a sense of urgency. Stop signs and traffic lights became mere suggestions as he raced us toward the local hospital, just 30 minutes away. Amid the chaotic drive, I found myself surprisingly silent, focusing solely on reaching the hospital as quickly as possible and breathing through every contraction as they quickly came and went. Each turn and bump in the road only amplified the pain I was experiencing, unaware that our second baby was already crowning and making their grand entrance into the world, ready to join us. AHHHHHHHHHHH!

We finally arrived in a record-breaking time, of course, and as I gathered my composure, took a giant deep breath and stood up to exit the truck, I frantically crossed my legs and screamed out. "It's coming out right now!!!!!". I felt immense pressure below, almost like a watermelon was rimming my uterus and wanting to drop out. I screamed out to Mark that I was unable to walk, so he quickly went into overdrive and searched for the closest wheelchair and raced it over to me. We rushed to labour and delivery triage, and upon reaching reception, the nurses began their routine protocol questions, which seemed to stretch on for an eternity. Unable to contain myself, I did something quite out of character and let out a loud scream, exclaiming, "This baby is coming out right now!"

They seemed taken aback by how advanced my labour was. This seemed to put them in overdrive and they rushed me over to the nearest empty room closest to the triage desk. As the vaginal pressure continued to escalate and I became quickly aware of the situation unfolding. Feeling an urgent need to ensure my birth plan was followed, I exclaimed, "Can someone please get me an epidural?" However, after an examination, the nurse chuckled and informed me, "Ma'am, you're already 8cm dilated, and it's time to push. You're way too far along." I couldn't discern if my excitement stemmed from the impending arrival of my little one or the realization that I had to endure intense contractions and push without pain relief. To complicate matters further, the midwife I had seen throughout my pregnancy didn't have enough time to arrive, forcing us to make a spontaneous decision to proceed without her. Though unsettling, only four significant, excruciating pushes later, our second baby graced us with her lovely presence at 2:33 am, weighing 8lbs 3 oz and measuring 21 inches long. Our doctor looked up at Mark and me and said, "A beautiful little princess." **We both burst into tears and truly felt overjoyed and blessed that God had granted us the most perfect and healthy baby girl. She passed the APGAR scores with flying colours, and we took one good look at her and instantly felt that "OLIVIA" would be the best name for her. Olivia looked like an angel and little did we know she became our earth angel in the flesh. "Welcome to our family, baby girl!"**

Bringing Olivia home to Julian, who was 21 months old, stirred different emotions in both Mark and I. I was overwhelmed with joy and thrilled beyond measure at the prospect of having a daughter – a mini-me and a princess joining our little clan. In contrast, Mark found himself grappling with the concept of becoming a father to a little girl. As someone who had always embraced a robust sense of masculinity through sports, dirt biking, boating, snowmobiling, and more, the idea of having a girl in the household invoked a sense of solemn reflection within him. He often said, "What do I do with this little girl? I don't even know where to begin." I admired his brutal honesty and his vulnerability, but that wasn't making the transition into a family of four any easier. As the days passed, Olivia ate, slept, grew and repeated. She was a very well-adjusted baby, which made it easier for me as parenting two children under the age of 2, had its set of challenges. She effortlessly reached all her developmental milestones, and her beauty was undeniably striking. Wherever we ventured, it seemed as though someone would pause and approach us, unable to resist commenting on her beautiful face. Her big brown eyes always looked so alert and full of life, as though they were always telling us a story. These were happy moments in my life that, today, I often forget. I sometimes felt guilty that I was too blessed to have this so-called "million-dollar family." Having the perfect family with a healthy boy and girl. I often prayed during breastfeeds when I had so much time to reflect. I would thank the good heavens above, simply asking God, "Why am I so lucky? *I must have done something right in my life to have been granted something so grand." Who would have thought that only six short months later, I would be in a completely different predicament,* where I was at mental war with God and pleading that the outcome would be different? Was this a foreshadowing of what was about to unfold? Was I going to be punished for feeling so grateful that my life felt so perfect? Only time will tell as Olivia's story unravels.

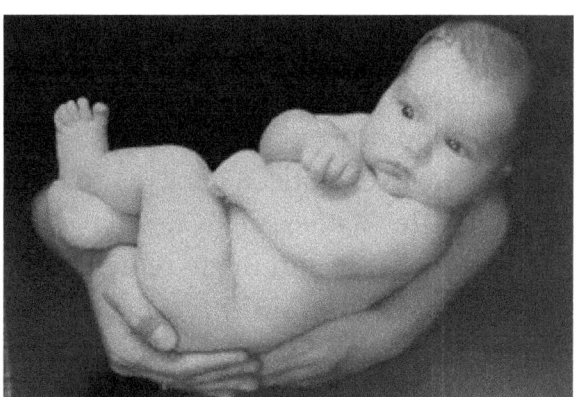

Olivia at 3 weeks old

TORN BETWEEN FEAR AND FAITH

Fast forward to 6 months later, my parents were over as usual, spending time with their beloved grandchildren. I thoroughly enjoyed their visits, as I would regain a bit of normalcy in my life, like a simple hot shower or an uninterrupted cup of coffee. Those were true luxuries for a new mom. My dad, overly analytical as he was; always noticed things way before anyone else did, which often annoyed us, and most of the time he was right. During their visit that day, he observed Olivia exhibiting unusual involuntary movements with her arms while she sat contentedly in her favourite bouncy chair. He noticed her lifting both arms simultaneously and lowering them one after the other. As these movements persisted over time, he couldn't shake the feeling that they were not typical for a baby, prompting him to address what he had observed. We instantly dismissed the notion that something was wrong and alluded to the fact that it was nothing more than bad digestion or a startle while sleeping. As most sleep-deprived parents are overly sensitive, the thought of having something wrong with the perfect baby was simply inconceivable. However, naturally, we all started to pay a bit more attention at that point to Olivia's behaviour, and unfortunately, the episode of her startles continued. At times we even noticed her eyes rolling back during the episode. In fact, after witnessing a few days' worth of these episodes, we witnessed her beginning to regress in her skills. She was no longer smiling, nor would she reach out to her toys above her bouncy chair. She seemed a lot more dazed and confused and would stare into thin air without blinking for minutes at a time. My brother commented once when he was visiting, on how talented he thought she was for being able to participate in long staring contests with him and win every time. Little did we know what was yet to unravel. Realizing it was time to seek prompt medical advice for our daughter, we visited her pediatrician the following day. We described what we had observed, only to be reassured by the physician that we were likely overreacting. She suggested it might be the "MORO REFLEX," a common experience for most infants between 3-6 months of age. This reflex involves the baby throwing back their head, extending their arms and legs, and then pulling the arms inward, typically occurring in response to a sudden loss of support. Receiving the reassuring information from the pediatrician brought immense relief, as any new parents would feel. We returned home, still vigilant for any unusual behavioural signs. However, our relief was short-lived as, a few days later, we noticed the involuntary movements returning, particularly after she woke from a nap, and this time, they were more intense and frequent. Concerned about the escalation, we knew something was seriously wrong, prompting the need for immediate medical attention. In a state of intense emotions, we reached out to our 24-hour telehealth line. After hearing our description, they urgently instructed us to visit our local children's hospital for further assessment. Terrified, our emotions overwhelmed us as we prepared to seek professional help for our daughter. *A million thoughts raced through our minds, leaving us feeling helpless. At that moment, the only thing that seemed logical was to pray. So, I began to pray. I prayed and prayed and prayed, hoping for a positive outcome.*

LIANA CANCIAN

FEELING SUCKERPUNCHED

December 4, 2006, remains a day etched in my memory—a day I wish to erase from my distant recollections forever. On that fateful day, we brought Olivia to Sick Kids Hospital, our local children's hospital in Toronto. The initial examination involved the first on-call physician and the on-site staff neurologist. After conducting an EEG and reviewing the results that night, we received the most devastating news any parent dreads. Our seemingly perfect little girl was not as perfect as we had believed. The jerks we observed were not in fact the MORO REFLEX but seizures, yes….seizures. They were specifically called Infantile Spasms (IS), also known as WEST SYNDROME.

The revelation left us with a barrage of questions. What were infantile spasms? Why did she experience them? Would they eventually fade with time? How could they be treated? These questions swirled through our minds amid the overwhelming shock. The physician explained the characteristics of IS, emphasizing their association with waking up from sleep. During an episode, the body's muscles stiffen, often bending forward like a jackknife, with knees pulled up and arms thrown out to the side. While he couldn't pinpoint the cause of Olivia's IS, he clarified that IS was merely a symptom of an underlying issue in the body. A problem that could arise from brain development in the womb, an infection, a brain injury, or abnormal blood vessels, among other possibilities. What?! My mind was reeling with uncertainty and guilt, questioning what I might have done to cause this. I was left speechless, feeling utterly sick to my stomach, and the look on my husband's face mirrored my shock. The physician stressed the urgency of further investigation to uncover this symptom's root cause and swiftly control it. We struggled to process the overwhelming news delivered to us, feeling like a deer in headlights with no clear direction for navigating this unexpected turn of events.

Meanwhile, we were sent home with a prescription for VIGABATRIN, also known as Sabril, recognized as the first-line treatment for IS. The physician explained that this initial treatment typically had the highest success rate in controlling seizures. However, he cautioned that if this course of action proved ineffective, the efficacy of subsequent treatment options diminished. As I listened to the physician's explanation, a glimmer of hope clung to my heart, desperately yearning for this medication to be the solution. I wished for it to defeat those agonizing spasms and, above all, to restore my baby to her former self, the baby girl I once knew, happy, playful and free.

The realization that my innocent baby would now have to rely on daily medication, potentially for the rest of her life, instilled a deep sense of terror within me. I was broken and shattered into a million pieces…

We left the pharmacy feeling deflated, as though we were sucker punched. A night I never want to recall, but little did I know, it was just the beginning of what was yet to come.

THE CALM BEFORE THE STORM

Our next step was the painful waiting game. We were waiting for MRI test results to further determine the cause of these seizures. As difficult as it was to process, each of us handled it quite differently. Mark is a factual, "black-and-white" kind of a guy who spent countless hours on his IMAC googling the terms seizures, causes and prognosis, only to come up with grim outcomes. In comparison, I chose to stay away from the internet and remain hopeful by relying on the company of my friends and family and my prayers to hope for a positive outcome. I held onto optimism, believing this was a temporary blip in her otherwise beautiful, long, and healthy life. I prayed that the medication she was receiving would stop the dreadful infantile spasms and help her regain what she had lost. Hearing positive stories of children outgrowing seizures, I continued to hope and pray that Olivia would be one of those success stories. Although many studies showed that children who suffer seizures at such a young age often have a bleaker prognosis, I chose to believe that anything was possible and that we were going to defy the odds. After being on the new drug for over a week, we were overjoyed to see Olivia start to finally re-learn her lost skills. Seeing her roll over again, coo and reach out to grab her toys brought pure joy into our hearts. Seeing her beautiful smile return was something we had been longing for since that feeling of being sucker-punched. We were starting to feel more positive and hopeful we had taken a turn for the better. Soon we could put this dreadful nightmare behind us and hope to chat about it over coffee in years to come. We hung on tight to this beautiful notion that our baby was getting better and, hopefully, this upcoming MRI would be clear and show no evidence of any life-altering ailments. *We placed our mental bets on science and hoped this positive outcome would continue and work in our favour. It was our calm that we needed to help us gain our strength, regroup our feelings and feel happiness in our hearts again, which had been absent for weeks. We needed this more than we knew it!*

UNRAVELLING THE UNCONTROLLABLE: FACING THE DIAGNOSIS

On December 26, 2006, Boxing Day, we had scheduled tests for Olivia – an MRI and an EEG – with the hope of uncovering the root cause of the distressing infantile spasms she was enduring. Traditionally, Boxing Day held a joyful significance for us. It was often spent lounging in pyjamas all day, unwinding, arranging new toys for Julian and simply appreciating all of our fortunes. It was a time of overwhelming gratitude and feeling blessed for all we had. However, on this particular day, the atmosphere was the complete opposite. It was filled with nervousness and uncertainty. Instead of feeling blessed, I grappled with inner conflicts, waging wars with "MY GOD." Gratitude was certainly not at the top of my list, to say the least.

The day commenced early with Olivia undergoing a sedated MRI, followed by an EEG, renal ultrasound, and cardiac echogram. It was a lot for a little one to endure, however we were all determined to find answers. Completing these tests was crucial for gaining clarity and, hopefully, a favourable prognosis. Olivia, as always, was remarkable and cooperative, almost as if she intuitively knew what lay ahead. Meanwhile, we were a bundle of nerves, putting on a brave front and trying to stay positive for each other, even as we grappled with the possibility of unfavourable results lurking beneath the surface.

After spending half the day on tests and anxiously awaiting results, we forced ourselves to have a bite to eat in the cafeteria.

Little did we know this would be our last normal meal before our lives changed forever. Later, we were summoned into the clinic room to await a discussion with the neurologist. Sitting side by side on an uncomfortable blue polyester cold couch, we shared a sombre silence, watching Olivia peacefully fall asleep in her stroller. It felt like the perfect calm before the storm, a moment of tranquillity before facing the potentially life-altering news. The neurologist entered the room accompanied by a group of student physicians wearing a troubled expression. At that moment, an unspoken understanding passed between us, signalling that the news might be unfavourable.

Holding our breath, we awaited the revelation. The neurologist began by informing us that our perfect daughter, whom we believed to be a blessing, had now become merely a statistic. Based on the test results, she diagnosed her with a sporadic genetic disease leading to the growth of benign tumours on her brain and potentially on various areas of her body. These tumours were identified as "TUBERS," and the condition was termed "TUBEROUS SCLEROSIS (TS)." The neurologist explained that these tubers were causing interference in the brain, leading to the infantile spasms she was experiencing. Left untreated, these spasms could result in severe developmental delays, intellectual disability, and lifelong epilepsy. I was utterly speechless as if an unexpected blow had knocked my breath out. No amount of preparation could have readied me for the heart-wrenching gravity of this situation. Meanwhile, Mark wore a weighty expression, his face etched with anger and a profound sense of betrayal. Perhaps it was all too overwhelming for him, stirring up haunting emotions from eight short years ago when he received the devastating news of his 20-year-old brother's tragic motorcycle accident. We were tormented with so many questions: Why is this happening to us?

What did we do to deserve this in our life? Every past wrongdoing flashed before our eyes as we tried to make sense of whether it could possibly equate to this dreadful news.

After holding our breaths with shock and finally taking in a puff of stale air, reluctantly returned to our horrible new reality. The neurologist explained how vital and crucial it was to obtain complete control of her seizures as quickly as possible so that she didn't fall further behind in her development. Since her seizures seemed better controlled upon starting her meds, we had a glimpse of hope. However, her prognosis was unknown as it was mainly based on how well her seizures would stay controlled, as it varied from child to child. She continued explaining that she may be a candidate for surgery, but it would require time for her brain to grow and develop before they even entertained the idea. Although the surgery was terrifying and difficult to digest at that moment, it offered a smidge of hope that this could be an option, giving her a chance to live a better quality of life. I hung on to that notion and kept the idea near and dear to my heart, as though that was the only shred of optimism I had heard all day. I knew that day forward that the hospital's phone number would unfortunately forever be ingrained in my brain. I knew I was now unfavourably tied to this god-forsaken place, to this building, to this department and to these doctors. Even if I wanted to run away and hide from what had just punched us in the face, I knew we needed them more than they needed us. This day marked the beginning of a new life for her and us. A life that we knew nothing of or even knew how to navigate. It appeared as if all our hopes and dreams for Olivia's future lay shattered on the floor of that cold, sterile clinical room, left to perish in despair.

Could we ever live a happy life again? Were we up to the challenge of handling all the upcoming hurdles while keeping it together? Could we ever see the beauty of life again after this day? Having an "A-Type" personality made things even more challenging to fathom this idea: *I had no control over her outcome or destiny. It was OLIVIA against the WORLD. We were just bystanders watching her life about to unfold and only time would tell the outcome!*

REDEFINING RESILIENCE

As months unfolded, our family experienced the usual ups and downs typical of households with young kids. Yet, the additional strain of vigilantly monitoring Olivia day after day took a toll on all of us. Life post-December 26th became an uncharted territory. I began keeping a journal, meticulously documenting her daily seizures while tracking her developmental progress and milestones. It seemed so sad that I was writing down more seizure activity day to day than all her gains and milestones being met, as normal babies have. Although she achieved milestones, they came at a noticeably slower pace.

With the guidance of a developmental pediatrician from our local agency, we underwent regular monitoring to assess her progress. By the time Olivia turned 12 months, she had started crawling and rolling over in her bed. Despite being significantly behind her peers, we were overjoyed at her accomplishments!

Witnessing any kind of acquired skill from Olivia at this point was reassuring. I secretly hoped she would soon "catch up and be "normal" or simply "fit in." However, watching other children at similar ages flourish and effortlessly surpass milestones, I had a new struggle on my hands that I had to learn to endure and overcome. It wasn't easy!! I wanted so much to be happy for my friend's children as they began effortlessly learning to walk, run, and do the things that toddlers do, but again, the demon inside me begged to differ. My friends and neighbours were always so important to me, and as social as I was, I struggled many days to get myself off the "pity train" and join them in their playgroups. As much as you tell yourself that we shouldn't compare, the force is larger than life. We are human, and it is a normal process of human cognition. I wanted so much to be happy, to enjoy my child at whatever stage she encountered. I often recited that "I will love and accept Olivia for who she is and not what she cannot do," however, believing it was the challenge. How can we care and love someone so much yet feel so disappointed, as though we got the shit end of a stick? I am sure my husband had his own demons to deal with, and watching Olivia fall behind only added fuel to his own personal fire. He knew that the two of us going down this slippery slope of self-loathing would not end well for anyone, including our children's well-being. He quickly learned to bury his own feelings while encouraging me to end the self-pity party and start accepting Olivia for who she was. To me, it was easier said than done. I think I felt at that time that if I started to accept Olivia with challenges and all, I was giving up the battle of trying to help her. However, as time went on, I persisted in holding onto hope. Despite the negative thoughts plaguing me, I decided to stay busy. Going against my natural inclination, I immersed myself in local mommy groups and sought to remain as active as possible. I aimed to keep my mind occupied, hoping it would be too preoccupied to engage in internal battles.

My new motto was to stop overthinking the "what ifs" and start doing it! Although it felt impossible at times, it seemed it was what I needed most; to face the dragon head-on. I needed to get out there and face adversity. I needed to see that other families shared their challenges too and that it wasn't just me struggling.

Little did I realize at that time I was unknowingly preparing myself for the challenges that lay ahead. By facing my own weaknesses and seeking out new tools for personal growth, I was laying a solid foundation within myself. I was learning the invaluable skill of accepting the unacceptable, embracing vulnerability and letting go of fear. It was a process of developing resilience and building a tough exterior, one that began when I started opening up and sharing my raw stories of heartache without fearing judgment from others. Throughout this journey, Olivia continued to experience seizures, but I was determined not to let her be defined solely by her disability. ***Perhaps it was my inherent nature or my unwavering determination to avoid spiralling into despair, but what I needed most to survive was the presence of people who loved and cared for me. Their support and unconditional love became my lifeline during the most trying times.***

BEHIND THE MASK OF DIGNITY

Finding effective seizure control for Olivia while ensuring her developmental progress became our greatest hurdle. By the time she reached 15 months old, she had already gone through multiple treatments, none of which provided significant relief from her seizures. She experienced around 5-6 seizures per day, often occurring upon waking. These seizures varied in intensity, ranging from subtle eye twitches that could easily go unnoticed to full-body jerks and twitching lasting several minutes. Each episode shattered my heart as I watched Olivia struggle, feeling utterly powerless to alleviate her suffering. To spare our loved ones from witnessing the distressing sight of seizures, I often kept Olivia away, shielding them from the overwhelming feelings of anger and sadness that consumed me. I was resolute in my determination to protect her from the world while also safeguarding any dreams they may have had for her. Though concealing these episodes was challenging, it provided a shield against the unanswerable questions and the pity that would only deepen my burden. Behind each episode, as I emerged from my refuge away from loved ones - often the bathroom - I would put on a brave face, pretending nothing had happened. It took immense strength to preserve our remaining dignity. The burden felt overwhelming, and I often grappled with a sense of isolation, knowing that no one else truly understood the magnitude of our pain. Shielding Olivia from a critical and judgmental world became a coping mechanism, a necessary act of self-preservation. While our family meant well and cared deeply for us, the weight of this struggle was ours to carry, slowly chipping away at our very souls. ***Many times, I found myself sitting on the bathroom floor, tears streaming down my face, feeling utterly helpless as I cradled Olivia in my arms. I would plead to the heavens above, praying fervently for each seizure to be the last, willing to do absolutely anything in exchange for her health.***

BEYOND THE PRESCRIPTION

As desperation set in, we found ourselves diverging in our views and beliefs regarding Olivia's disability and the approach to her treatment. I became increasingly open to exploring any possible avenue that could offer relief from her seizures, willing to try anything that could give her brain much-needed respite. On the other hand, Mark held steadfast in his confidence in Western medicine and trusted that Olivia was in the right place, despite its failures thus far. It was at this point that my journey led me to delve into Eastern medicine. I sought out an assertive Asian doctor who strongly believed in the healing power of acupuncture. Placing my trust in his hands, we pursued months of treatment for Olivia who was at the tender age of 10 months, only to see minimal to no improvement. Driven by my unwavering determination to find a solution for Olivia, I delved into the world of naturopathy. It was during this exploration that I stumbled upon a specialized clinic in Burlington catering to children with special needs and autism. Intrigued by their approach, I followed their recommendation to modify Olivia's diet and incorporate supplements. Adopting a gluten and casein-free diet for months seemed to have had a positive impact on her alertness and well-being, but unfortunately, it did not bring the desired control over her seizures. Despite the continued disappointments, my willingness to try any possibility that held promise remained constant. I was ready to explore every avenue that could potentially enhance Olivia's overall quality of life. Each setback only fueled my determination to keep searching for answers. It was my fight to fight, even if I was doing it alone. I wasn't going to give up, no matter how much it consumed me!

You see, my husband Mark often referred to me as a "dreamer", a "non-realist", when in fact I felt my actions were solely a result of my having hope. As long as I had hoped, I was willing to try new things. After all, how would I know if anything would ever work? I wanted to leave no stone unturned and wanted to feel so confident in myself that I did everything in my physical power while I was Olivia's mom on this earth to help her in any way I could, even if the odds were stacked against us. I guess secretly, I really wanted her to be better, to be fixed and to be rid of those dreadful seizures, so she could catch up with her toddler peers and blend in. I probably wasn't ready at that point to accept that she was different. I didn't like being at the mercy of Western medicine to help us because it disappointed us time and time again. Maybe Mark was right? Perhaps all along I wished to change something that I absolutely had no control over. He always said, "We must stop trying to change Olivia and start loving and accepting who she was". I felt I was giving up or throwing in the towel if I did just that, but maybe there was some validity to that statement. Perhaps he did have a point, but I wasn't ready to accept it. Not just yet! At this point, Olivia's development continued at a snail's pace, and her spasms worsened more alarmingly. Most of her skills acquired up to that point were slowly vanishing. Her babbling, smiling, reaching out to grab her toys, eye tracking, and, most of all, her happy spirit was fading underneath our nose as though we were slowly losing her to a viscous whirlwind of seizures. It was as though this ferocious animal unleashed inside her, creating havoc on her beautiful and peaceful little soul. We felt so many emotions with no experience to support or guide us. The helplessness and rage were all too real. ***Our inner happiness was being buried further and further into our souls. We found it difficult to feel grateful most days, but our determination not to give up on Olivia helped us push through and persevere.***

A BEACON IN THE DARKNESS

At our next follow-up appointment, we all came to the agreement with our pediatric neurologist that our current seizure meds were failing us and that the next step was to commence a very aggressive steroid treatment called ACTH, also known as Adrenocorticotropic hormone therapy. This offered much improvement in seizure control, even in the most difficult-to-control epilepsy. This treatment is now the first line of treatment for IS, but unfortunately, it wasn't many years ago. Therefore, the decision was pretty clear, and we knew we had to bite the bullet and take on this new opportunity in Olivia's quest to find seizure cessation. We were desperate and exhausted, in dire need of a solution, and quickly. With each passing day, we were bidding farewell to all the beautiful milestones she had worked so hard to achieve. For every step forward she took, a seizure would push her back five steps. Witnessing it was excruciating for us as parents. We knew it was time to explore the next treatment option, even if it meant opting for a more aggressive approach.

The treatment plan demanded three months of injections, administered at home by a nurse every other day. The potential side effects loomed large: weight gain, high blood pressure, and increased irritability. Yet, we stood ready. It was as if we wore blinders, heedless of any cautionary advice. There was no luxury of time for contemplation or reflection. The clock ticked relentlessly, and time was not on our side. Olivia needed to reclaim her path, and we were determined to bid farewell to those spasms for good finally. We were optimistic after the appointment and went home with hope in our hearts that this would do it!!

On October 1, 2007, at the tender age of only 17 months, Olivia began her ACTH steroid treatment journey. The initial injection was administered by an extraordinary nurse by the name of Grace. Her warmth and friendliness were truly exceptional. Grace approached her responsibilities with abundant compassion, gentleness, and care, not only for Olivia but also for us as parents. She clearly possessed a genuine passion for her work, making it seem effortless and incredibly rewarding. It was as if she were destined for this role. We developed a deep appreciation for her presence in our lives. In fact, we eagerly anticipated our encounters with her, and little did we realize just how much we relied on her support and kindness. She became a ray of light during an otherwise dark and challenging time, providing us with the strength and reassurance we needed.

The initial injections seemed relatively manageable, aside from the soreness Olivia experienced at the injection site on her upper legs. However, little did we know what lay ahead. Determined to stay optimistic, we remained committed to the treatment, continuing with each administered injection. But as time went on, unexpected challenges arose. Olivia's body began to retain water, a lot of water, causing her weight to increase rapidly. She had gained a whopping 10 lbs of water to a little body that was only 20 lbs. This caused her great discomfort which then manifested into extreme irritability, and she spent much of her days and nights crying in misery. It was heart-wrenching to witness her discomfort and inability to find relief. All the skills she had learned up to that point seemed to fade away, and she appeared incredibly uncomfortable in her own skin. This constant state of distress took a toll not only on Olivia but also on our entire family. In an attempt to provide her with some comfort, Olivia spent her nights in a stroller beside my bed, where I would gently rock her back and forth while trying to fall asleep. This seemed to offer her a short period of relief and provided us with an opportunity to catch up on the much-needed sleep we had been deprived of.

It was clear that Julian was feeling neglected during those challenging days. Balancing the needs and wants of my 2.5-year-old son, who desired to build Lego houses and go on bike rides, with the constant demands of caring for a screaming baby was incredibly difficult. I made the tough decision to enroll Julian in a local Montessori school a couple of days a week. While guilt weighed heavily on me, it was a necessary step to help me cope with the overwhelming circumstances. I needed to find a way to make it through each day in one piece. Julian required more than I could offer him at that moment. He deserved a sense of normalcy beyond our home, away from the constant crying, medical interventions, and adapted toys catering to Olivia's needs. Although sending Julian to school posed risks due to Olivia's compromised immune system, it was our best decision. Sometimes, the right choice isn't easy, but navigating new challenges and seeking alternative routes has imparted invaluable lessons and instilled hope for a brighter future.

During that challenging period, we also made the decision to hire a nanny to assist us in caring for Olivia. This choice provided some much-needed relief and allowed me to devote more time to my son, who had silently endured the difficulties we faced. That was when we hired Mona, a Filipino nanny who quickly became our lifeline, an earthly angel who brought light into our lives. I made it a practice to find the silver lining in every dreadful situation, and having her support was a true blessing. It felt as if God had sent her to me when I needed her the most. Her presence reminded me that even in the darkest times, there is always some good that can emerge. She became the guiding light that led me through the long, dark corridor, even when I felt lost and wanted to give up. She held the torch, illuminating the way.

In the midst of everything that was going on, we stumbled upon a remarkable discovery: eating became Olivia's ultimate source of joy during her treatments. Those moments when she sat in her highchair, relishing her meals, became our absolute happiest times. It didn't matter what she ate; she embraced it with enthusiasm. Every bite she took seemed like she had been deprived of food for days.

These fleeting moments of happiness allowed us to momentarily escape the challenges we faced. We were completely absorbed in the smallest details that brought us immense joy. It was as if these moments were tiny fragments of pure bliss that effortlessly dissolved all our worries and troubles.

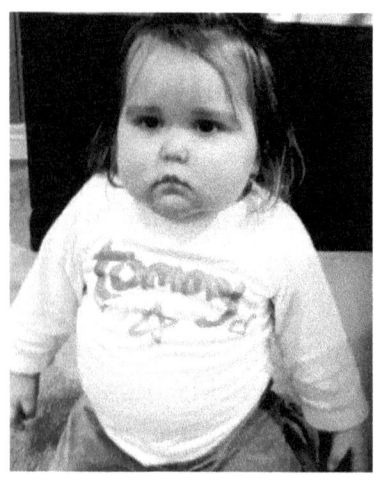

Olivia after being on ACTH steroid treatment for 4 weeks and had already gained 5 lbs of water

Mona with Olivia (18 months) and Julian (3)

JUGGLING GRIEF AND GRATITUDE

Upon completing Olivia's steroid treatment, we had a surprisingly great breakthrough period with no seizures. It was the best I had ever seen her. She was vital, vibrant, and full of life and watching her be her happy and joyful little self brought warmth to my inner soul. She was the "real" Olivia **shining through** ever so bright, without the cloud of confusion and daze that had once taken over her little brain from the array of electrical misfirings. It was so refreshing to see Olivia's true personality return, but for how long? The unsettling feeling that this could be over too soon and we could be back to that terrible place we once were, was hard to fathom.

We tried hard to swallow the uncertainties and enjoy every moment of Olivia's good days without thinking about the what-ifs. Olivia began re-learning her lost skills at an alarming rate. Walking, babbling, jumping, playing on playsets, everything most neurotypical toddlers were doing, filled our days. We even taught her to use the potty, which I thought impossible. Although she was still behind most of her peers, she progressed in leaps and bounds. It was "our high," our time to remember what happiness felt like. It was exactly what we needed to recharge our batteries, take a deep breath, and prepare ourselves for the uncertain future. We cherished those moments so greatly. It was the smallest things that meant the world to us. Our normal was different than most, but we slowly embraced this new world, one hurdle at a time. We had many great days and a handful of bad days, including returning seizures. It was almost as though it was a harsh reminder of how dreadful epilepsy can be. It felt like a balancing act, and we were the magicians. Trying to balance the days we felt so grateful with the days that grief could cut us like a knife. I stumbled across a few books in those days that many friends would kindly suggest but rarely had time to read. However, this quote from one of the books stood out vividly, which I will never forget. It was by Francis Weller, who wrote a book called "Grief." "The work of the mature person is to carry grief in one hand and gratitude in the other and to be stretched large by them. How much sorrow can I hold? That's how much gratitude I can give". It perfectly depicted my life and how I had felt most days. One of my hands holds the grief, which includes everything I thought I lost or wished I had for Olivia. Wishing she had a healthy and functional brain. Wishing she had a better quality of life without suffering from daily seizures and missing out on the world around her. We often felt saddened by what we had lost, our own personal freedoms. We felt like we were instantly thrown into this lifelong caregiver role that most parents don't sign up for. The notion that Olivia may never get married or bear her own children was heart-wrenching. We had to come to terms with this harsh reality that Olivia may never even live independently and that she may one day outlive us, leading us to a whole new world of uncertainties. On the flip side, according to Weller, the other hand holds all that I am grateful for. I often struggled with this concept and had difficulty coming up with anything that made me feel remotely grateful. However, as I tried to focus on what surrounded me that was good, my family, my friends, my own health, and my community, I began to fill my gratitude cup naturally. Some days were easier than others, and it was often a challenge to zero in on the goodness that surrounded me. I often said that my mom's prayers gave me the strength and perseverance to help me get through my days and move forward.

Weller explains that if one hand is empty, the other becomes overwhelmed, weakens and may often collapse. He articulates how we must hold gratitude and grief as equals. The hands need to support and build one another rather than cancel each other out. As much as I found it difficult to digest this notion, I decided to write it down with hopes that one day it would resonate and make sense. I knew that when things got tough, I could count on this quote and find solace in his words.

I am now slowly understanding and after having a phone conversation with another mother of a child with TS, it makes sense to me now.

The week I received Olivia's diagnosis, I was naturally devastated and determined to talk to any parent going through this similar journey with the hopes that it would provide me with some support. The hospital helped me connect with a lovely woman who lived on the eastern coast of Canada and had a 10 yr old daughter diagnosed with TS. I instantly thought this was a terrific idea as she could shed some light on the last ten years since her daughter's diagnosis and prepare me for what to expect. I hoped to hear some positive and reassuring news that could lend a shimmer of hope which was what I needed most. Naturally, as a worried parent, I bombarded her with many questions regarding her child's prognosis and development. She was lovely, caring and quite patient with my many inquiries. She knew I was coming from a scared and heartbroken place, so she tread lightly and tried to comfort me by taking the time to answer all my questions in the most eloquent way possible. She explained that *"everyone diagnosed with TS is very different. No two individuals are alike".* With this being said, she explained that *"Olivia will go through many hurdles in life, and unfortunately, those struggles are essential for you to accept where she will be developmentally in the future. Jumping ahead ten years to grab a glimpse of where your child will be can only be heartbreaking. The years of experience build up our appreciation, love and respect for these special beings".* WOW!! When I heard that, I didn't know if I should cry in disbelief or just graciously thank her for her sincerity. I wished at that very moment, I could jump through that phone to give her the biggest hug I could offer. It was what I needed most, and she was there to guide me!! With this advice, I now can understand the validity of what Weller meant in his quote—having to navigate through Olivia's journey to appreciate the simple things that she accomplishes. It may have been as simple as her first step on her own or listening to her humming to her favourite wiggles tune in her sweet little voice in the backseat of my SUV. Only after this phone conversation did I feel my hand slowly filling with gratitude. **Becoming vulnerable and opening myself up freely to people sharing this similar journey was the key to my coping. We cannot do this alone. It allowed me to put one foot in front of the other and move on. I knew the challenge of balancing grief and gratitude would be a lifelong journey that would begin with acceptance. I was definitely up for the challenge.**

A TIME TO HEAL

Olivia had a long break in seizures since her steroid treatment at the age of 16 months. She went five to six months with neither a twitch, jerk or blank stare, and it gave her brain such a great chance to heal. This time allowed her developing mind to create new synapses and strengthen any newly acquired skills. The more days passed without a seizure, the more Olivia had a chance to move forward in development and catch up for lost time. During this period, Olivia achieved significant milestones. She mastered the skill of toileting and started walking independently by the age of 22 months. This marked a tremendous achievement for us, especially considering moments, in our darkness moments, when we doubted if these skills were attainable. Filled with joy and anticipation for her future, we were over the moon. Olivia also developed a keen interest in her alphabet, numbers, and nursery rhymes. A day wouldn't go by without her reciting every song she learned from her WIGGLES videos with just the right musical pitch, and her memory was surprisingly enhanced. It was baffling to see Olivia struggle to form sentences, yet she displayed an extraordinary understanding of the alphabet's sounds. While it was a phenomenon, we embraced whatever her young mind could offer. Olivia became acquainted with various animal sounds, often mimicking them as we passed by farms. She could express her needs using learned phrases like "GOTTA GO PEE PEE IN THE POTTY" or "It's RAINING, WE NEED AN UMBRELLA," which brought immense joy to us. Hearing her soft little voice recite "Twinkle Twinkle Little Star" in the back seat became a cherished moment during our long drives, prompting us to turn off the radio to savour these special moments. It was a magical time for our family, marked by the utmost joy and a willingness to embrace it all. Olivia was rediscovering the world with fresh eyes, and we were eager to guide her journey. Witnessing her personality shine through during this seizure-free period was like glimpsing into her soul through her big brown eyes. Enrolling her in preschool at our local community center felt like the right step forward; she needed more than I could provide at home. With a support worker in place, we were thrilled to see Olivia embraced and included by her peers. However, she appeared no different physically; her ability to socialize and participate in activities required adaptation. Her infectious energy and radiant smile won over everyone, with teachers often remarking on the storytelling quality of her sparkling eyes. They felt it was a window into Olivia's innermost feelings, and I couldn't agree more.

Despite Olivia's difficulty articulating sentences, she exhibited echolalia, a behaviour where she repeated certain words throughout the day as her brain processed and absorbed new vocabulary. While it could be amusing at times, some may have found her word choices inappropriate. For example, her enthusiastic greeting of "POO POO" at school pickup might have raised eyebrows. I couldn't help but be overjoyed by Olivia's unique expression.

With seizures no longer weighing heavily on our minds, our days felt brighter and more manageable, as if a massive burden had been lifted. It was a beautiful period of feeling normal again and watching our children play and interact like siblings. Julian, in particular, benefited immensely from this newfound sense of normalcy.

We desperately needed a break—a chance for our bodies and minds to rejuvenate and recharge. Learning to appreciate life's smallest blessings as they arrived became an ongoing lesson, acknowledging the uncertainty of what tomorrow might bring.

The happy days when Olivia (2) was seizure free for a period of time.

Memories of Olivia during her 2nd year in 2008

SURGICAL CROSSROADS

Months came and went, and Olivia flourished gracefully amidst the perfect life's rhythm. Our days were predictable, and every day gladly rolled into the next, watching her blossom, and absorb life's wonders ever so beautifully. It was truly the most amazing time for us as parents and, of course, for her to be free of the dreadful electrical misfirings. Life was perfect as we knew it. However, hardship could not stray too far, and when Olivia was three, tragedy struck us ever tremendously as those atrocious seizures returned and this time with retaliation. As though Olivia was being punished for an act she never committed. ***How fair was this for her, for us? It was the beginning of the end of what had given us such great joy.*** She began having drop seizures, also known as "ATONIC SEIZURES." They would arrive unexpectedly with no warning on site and cause her to lose muscle strength, falling to the ground. This type of seizure was not only alarming but very unsettling for parents to witness and endure. It was just another thing to add to my watchlist. Throughout this rollercoaster journey, Olivia experienced her fair share of bumps and bruises from numerous falls. Monitoring her every move took a toll on my mental well-being, as I constantly worried about her safety. There were times when I missed seeing her fall, filling me with guilt for not being there to protect her. Then came the day when she collided with the corner of the bookshelf in our family room while I was briefly occupied in the bathroom. The loud thud and subsequent quiet whimper immediately alerted me that something was wrong. Hurrying to Olivia's side, I found her lying there with blood streaming down her forehead, yet remarkably, she didn't shed a tear. She looked up at me and said, "Ouchie," with a half smile. As her deep brown eyes filled with grief, her sentiments were ever so intact, almost emotionless. Did she not feel the pain? Was she unintentionally protecting herself from what the future had in store for her? Her reaction was quite shocking yet comforting at the same time. Knowing that she was not suffering and could endure what her body was experiencing was my inner peace and made it much easier for me to cope. She very rarely complained of pain, and we realized that she possibly had a very high threshold for pain, which we later found out was quite common for children with special needs. As we arrived at the emergency, she patiently sat on the bed smiling ear to ear, singing her favourite tunes while the doctor stitched her up. He couldn't believe how cooperative she was and commented on her radiating joy and contentment amidst all the chaos. This was when I began to believe that Olivia was extraordinary and had so many great qualities that we had yet to discover. At this point, I began to believe Olivia was blessed with angels who surrounded her and kept her calm and collected. Could it be her late uncle Allan holding her hand every step of the way or singing "Twinkle Twinkle" in her ear, keeping her calm? Her inner peace and gentle spirit made everyone near her feel so at ease. She made the job as parents and caregivers effortless. This event marked the beginning of many trips to the emergency from similar types of falls and adopting a helmet which became part of her new daily wardrobe. These so-called "drop seizures" became our newest dragon to defeat, so, with no choices, we were off to visit our neurologist, leaving her destiny in the hands of Western medicine yet again. The discussion with the neurology team was quite bleak. They explained that the honeymoon period for the steroid treatment was over, and the chances of any other drug being effective beyond this point became less and less. It led us to explore surgery as an option further. The last time we had this discussion, Olivia was only a year old and was not deemed a candidate due to her age and lack of brain development. Having to entertain this idea again was quite unnerving. However, as desperate as we were, we dove into the research head-on. We began to investigate our surgical options further. Surgery in Canada vs. surgery outside of Canada. Our rigorous research found a very aggressive, highly-acclaimed neurosurgeon by the name of Dr. Orrin Devinsky who headed out of a children's hospital in New York. He achieved remarkable success with bilateral brain resections, a procedure with its own set of high risks. Resecting both sides of the brain, where seizures originated from, offered a promising prognosis, but the chances of infection and potential minor paralysis were significant concerns. Given that Olivia's seizures originated from both sides of her brain naturally, this approach seemed like the most viable option. However, in Canada, the more common, conservative, and safer approach is known as unilateral brain resection, involving the removal of only one part of the brain in the hopes of eliminating the primary source of seizures.

However, the chance that seizures worsen or dissipate on the other side of the brain still exists. We spent our days and nights dissecting both options and investigating if our provincial insurance coverage would even cover such a horrendous medical bill of $175,000us if performed in the United States. An astronomical cost, but the stakes were high, and Olivia needed to be helped!! Our provincial medical insurance outlined that Olivia's surgery in the United States could be fully covered if she wasn't considered a surgical candidate in our home country. Determined to do what was best for Olivia, we found comfort in knowing that one of the world's leading children's hospitals was right here in our city of Toronto. We opted to begin the process at our local hospital, reserving the option to explore alternative options south of the border only if she didn't qualify for surgery locally.

From then on, Olivia underwent numerous tests to see if she would be the surgical candidate we hoped for. From CT scans and MRIs to PET scans and spinal taps, it was a month of rigorous testing, patience and resilience, and we hoped the outcome would land in our favour. Olivia was always calm and cooperative and truly made parenting her a breeze. We spent our days singing, playing and enjoying the peaceful country property while she wore her cute little pink helmet to prevent further injuries. We waited and waited and waited for answers from the neurology team, as they would meet weekly to discuss Olivia's surgical candidacy case. **We felt helpless, as though we were spectators sitting in the backseat of a theatre, watching Olivia's future unfold on stage while the doctors took turns playing the main role - God.** This decision would impact her life immensely, as it would determine the direction of where we were heading. Would we prefer to stay close to home and offer her a safer surgery that may not have the most optimal outcome, or did we courageously venture out to New York with no physical family to support us and take on a very aggressive surgical approach with higher risks involved but be faced with a better prognosis? We had a great deal at stake here, and as much as Mark crunched numbers and focused on the risks, *I couldn't help but focus and rely on the little faith I had left at that point. I pleaded to my God to guide and help me take on whatever challenge was next. Lately, my God wasn't in my good books. Nevertheless, when times got desperate, and I needed him most, faith was all I had to pull me through. Unsure if my prayers were truly heard or if I even believed in miracles, I surrendered myself as raw as I was, to a higher power, hoping for guidance and strength to face whatever challenges lay* *ahead and equip me with what I needed to cope and endure. It marked the start of a journey to restore my faith, a work in progress toward something greater, something profound.*

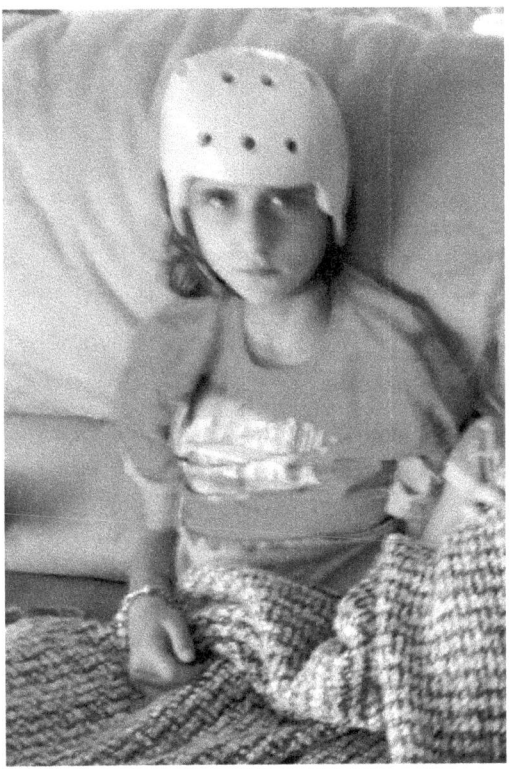

Olivia not happy as she wears her pink helmet for safety and protection from unexpected drop seizures

PUTTING TRUST IN SCIENCE

Mark and I sat there emotionless, with our anguished hearts in our throats, in that cold, sterilized clinic room, on a Monday in March 2009. We tried to make sense of all the medical terms being thrown at us from every direction by the neurology team as they explained the horrific details of Olivia's surgical journey. We were terrified at what it entailed. However, we knew it was necessary to defeat this dragon head-on. It was a very sharp double-edged sword that we were up against. They began by carefully reviewing the possibilities of seizure control due to a unilateral resection. They continued to present us with what they felt were great odds for her outcome. They explained how there would be an 80% chance of Olivia having at least 50% seizure control. At first, it was pretty difficult to digest the numbers presented to us as they didn't seem quite favourable. Upon further discussion and a better understanding of the severity of ongoing seizures and their effect on Olivia's brain and overall development, we knew we had to come to grips with this decision and accept this new obstacle with confidence. However, there was a potential risk we had to be aware of. Upon doing multiple EEGs and MRIs the team noticed an area of her brain that had ongoing seizures, and once removed, it posed a risk of affecting the function of her left hand. How can a parent who loves their child so deeply make a decision that could impact their child's physical appearance? The dilemma posed a formidable challenge. On the one hand, there was the prospect of Olivia potentially acquiring a physical disability in addition to her existing Tuberous Sclerosis diagnosis, with the potential for achieving a seizure-free status. On the other hand, the alternative was to forgo this risk, opting for minimal resection in the hope that seizures could be minimized. This decision had to be made on the day of surgery, a day fraught with despair and uncertainties, introducing a new hurdle to overcome. Placing unwavering trust in the team's expertise, supported by a globally recognized children's hospital, we were confident that Olivia's best interests were paramount. The goal was to eliminate any potential future regrets. Given the circumstances, we proceeded to schedule Olivia's surgery for a date in 2009.

We had to surrender and trust in the science and all the research, leaving no stone unturned, to ensure that Olivia received the best possible outcome - a tough pill to swallow but a collaborative decision made with honesty and confidence.

We learned that sometimes we must let go of our preconceptions and trust the experts and the research to make the best decisions for ourselves or our loved ones. It can be difficult to surrender control and accept a decision that may be hard to digest. Still, by being open, collaborative, and thorough in our decision-making process, we can have confidence that we have made the best possible choice.

GLORIOUS AWAKENING

Arriving in Toronto the day before Olivia's surgery, Mark and I opted to reserve a hotel close to the hospital in the city. This decision allowed us to be near Olivia during her recovery while providing us with a space for some much-needed downtime. We both were on edge, checking into our hotel and settling into our room, feeling like bundles of nerves. To distract ourselves and infuse positivity into our thoughts, we decided to make our last night together before the surgery enjoyable and memorable. Choosing to take Olivia for a leisurely stroll down Yonge St, one of the city's liveliest streets, seemed like the perfect plan. The sight of upscale shops and the activity of people bustling about was exactly the diversion we needed. Basking in the warm sun on our faces and relishing the delightful aroma from food trucks lining the streets, the atmosphere felt vibrant—just the right amount of diversion before the impending storm. As we pushed Olivia in her stroller, she smiled and seemed quite content as she happily clutched her favourite pink little monkey, providing her with much comfort. We needed so much to have time with one another before the rath began. In the days leading up to surgery, we couldn't ignore the remarkable change in Olivia's demeanor. As the doctors gradually tapered her medications over the past few days, Olivia's eyes glimmered with newfound brightness and awareness. It was as if she was emerging from a dark fog, seeing the world with fresh eyes and a renewed sense of clarity. For a fleeting moment, it felt reminiscent of the time she was seizure-free after her steroid treatment – a moment of pure joy and wonder. It was as though we were meeting Olivia for the first time, experiencing the delight of her presence without the burden of her diagnosis. This glimpse offered a compelling vision of what Olivia could have been without her medical struggles. It was like savouring a delicious fruit briefly before it vanished. Witnessing Olivia fully engaged with her surroundings, pointing and acknowledging things she wouldn't typically notice, was exhilarating. It was a refreshing reminder of her true colours and a testament to her resilience. She was talking up a storm and singing her little heart out. It was conflicting emotions of sadness and joy for us as we saw what the true Olivia was like in that three-and-a-half-year-old little body. We felt this time was priceless as we didn't know if we would ever see this side of her again. All we could do at that moment was savour every moment of Olivia's *glorious awakening;* and store it in our memory forever. Time was ticking, and the future of her health and well-being held so many unknowns. My thoughts spiralled out of control, and I urged myself to stop. These paralyzing thoughts weren't doing me any justice. I had to face the challenges head-on and prepare for what was about to untangle. ***Fear of the unknown crippled me, as I knew the harsh clutches of uncertainty all too well.*** The possibility of the upcoming surgery improving Olivia's condition and revealing more of her true self was a long-awaited hope and prayer for us. When we finally received news that the surgery was possible, it felt like an incredible gift we will always treasure. ***It was a powerful reminder that there could be a silver lining even amid struggle. This experience taught us to hold onto hope and never give up, even in adversity.***

IN THE HANDS OF HOPE

It was the day we dreaded for a long time - surgery day. What a roller coaster of emotions for Mark and me, to say the least. We couldn't believe that this day was finally here to torment us.

Upon reaching the second floor via the elevator, we found ourselves on the surgical deck. Any parent who has spent time at this hospital knows that the second and eighth floors are undesirable places to be. The eighth floor is where oncology patients receive treatment, and it's always a sombre and difficult environment for families.

Today we were heading to the 2nd floor, the next least favourable floor, the surgical ward. We were ready to join forces with families boarding the same ship of distress and uncertainty. We were leaving our precious children in the hands of our trusted doctors, who entered the pre-operative room so confident, mighty and almost God-like. Their appearance was quite the sight, covered from head to toe in light blue smocks, little hats and masks. No room for any flesh to show. Almost as though it was a clear depiction of how super-human and almost extra-terrestrial they were from the rest of us. As though a distinct reminder of how unique and vital they are to us in this world.

The surgeons ran over all the details of the surgery again and felt as though we were hearing it all for the very first time. Reminding us of all the risks involved added more fear and uncertainty to our extremely fragile state. Olivia, as sweet as she was, clutched her pink monkey and screamed out "crazy legs" and broke out in hysterics as she shook her favourite monkey's dangled legs back and forth, which brought a much-needed smile to our faces—a moment I will always cherish. It was the perfect comic relief for us. We comforted Olivia by singing her Twinkle and Twinkle in her ear. It was a special moment for us to remember how blessed we were to have such a sweet and innocent little girl—watching Olivia feel so happy and joyful during such sorrow and heartbreak. She was our earth angel, and she had no idea she was about to embark on a harrowing journey. How can a parent offer their final goodbyes to their sick children, and remain strong, yet crumbling with disheartenment on the inside? blatantly lying to our children that everything will be okay when, in fact, it was just the beginning of a long and challenging battle. What parents do and say in the name of their children's happiness and well-being is simply courageous and commendable. Where did we obtain such strength and bravery? Is it bestowed upon mothers from a higher being as we give birth and take on the role of parenting? Or is it a work in progress as we watch our children grow and build "tough skin" along the way? It was time for us to say goodbye. With tearful eyes, we pressed our last kisses onto Olivia's forehead, embracing her tightly and whispering our love into her ear. Mark and I clung to each other, overcome with emotion and heartache as the surgeons and nurses whisked her away. Olivia's small body occupied a fraction of the large hospital bed, surrounded by machines, wires, and surgical supplies. She held onto her pink monkey with innocent eyes, unaware of what she was about to endure. "Sweet dreams, Olivia," I whispered. "May they be filled with soaring butterflies and colourful flowers. We'll see you again soon. Very soon."

I looked over at my husband and saw him for the first time sobbing like a young schoolboy. An image I desperately wish I could banish from my mind eternally. Watching a strong man so powerful and in control of his feelings shatter into thousands of pieces before me. I quickly wiped away my tears, took his hand in mine, and knew, at that very moment, that it was my turn to be strong and led him to the waiting room. *We couldn't help but feel helpless and terrified at this moment. The surgeons were masters in their field, and we were indebted to them. We had to trust them open-heartedly and entirely that they had our children's best interests at heart. It was like the passing of the keys to a medical team that was now in the driver's seat dictating the route of Olivia's life journey.*

HEART IN HAND

PHASE ONE - BRAIN SURGERY

In the first surgery, the surgeons used an intraoperative neuronavigation system that helped to visualize the area and location of seizures for them to place a subdural electrode grid directly on her brain. By conducting this procedure and having this grid directly on her brain with no cranial distraction, they can effectively track and trace the precise location of where the seizure focus or seizures originate from. This procedure will assist the team in resecting the right focal point during the second phase of surgery. Therefore, once this grid was placed on Olivia's brain, they wrapped her head in gauze and sedated her. It was four long and painful days watching Olivia lay limp, unresponsive and strapped to a machine, which was recording and mapping her seizures through this sophisticated technology.

My appreciation for medical advancements and technology was at an all-time high. Watching as a parent, seeing Olivia's tiny body confined to an oversized hospital bed, with a fabric helmet secured to her head and wires protruding from the other end, was a difficult and distressing experience to undertake. By day three, a specialized team paraded in for further testing. They were responsible for mapping out Olivia's function for her extremities. Watching Olivia's fingers and feet move at the push of a computer button was simply remarkable. They were testing to see what parts of Olivia's brain were linked to vital bodily functions and making clear notes that would later assist them during the second surgery. It was a long four days, and seeing Olivia in a coma-like state, emotionless while being poked and prodded kept us on the edge of our seats with our **hearts in our hands.** Knowing her brain was fully exposed just underneath a thin layer of medical gauze was too difficult to bear. We just couldn't breathe until this whole ordeal was over. By the end of day four, the surgical team felt they had sufficient information gathered from the last few days of testing to create a successful surgical outcome. She was then scheduled for part two of the surgery the following day. While I sat there and watched Olivia's chest move up and down, reassuring me that she was still here with us, It was then that I decided to begin a blog that helped me share my deepest and darkest feelings while keeping our loved ones informed. It became my saving grace and the beginning of my cathartic journey.

That evening, by Olivia's bedside, hope and prayer hung heavily in the air, burdening our hearts. Tomorrow carried the anticipation of transformative change—a day when the trials, pain, and heartache might find purpose. As I sat beside her on the bed, I closed my eyes, cradling Olivia's tiny hand in mine, relishing the warmth of her delicate fingers. In my mind's eye, I pictured my little angel joyfully running through an expansive field adorned with daisies and butterflies, her radiant smile and deep brown eyes brimming with pure happiness. Clutching her beloved pink monkey in one arm and a handful of daisies in the other, the vision encapsulated a heartfelt longing for a future we hoped would come to fruition. Opening my eyes, the stark reality filled me with a profound sadness and an unshakeable love, a constant reminder of why we were enduring this challenging journey. We believed every moment spent fighting for Olivia's life would be justified by the promise of a happy ending.

As parents, our love for our children knows no bounds, and when faced with adversity, it only grows stronger. In those difficult and heartbreaking moments, we cling to what little hope we have and hold onto our unwavering devotion to our children; we draw on strength from the love that fuels us. We know that we must go on and believe in a better tomorrow.

PHASE TWO - BRAIN SURGERY

At 8:00 am, Olivia was taken in for her second phase of surgery. We didn't have a chance to look into her eyes and tell her how much we loved her or even say goodbye. It was difficult, but we gathered our strength and made our way to the surgical waiting room.

We plunged into a distressing waiting game upon entering the surgical waiting room. The atmosphere was saturated with an overpowering sense of despair, and the anxious expressions on the faces of families awaiting their loved ones' return from surgery remain etched in my memory. Their eyes mirrored a mixture of uncertainty and fear, a sentiment that resonated with our own experiences. It appeared as if each family was grappling with their own internal demons, contemplating the potential worst-case scenario if their child's surgery did not unfold successfully. As their child lies helpless on the operating table, under the bright lights and the influence of strong anesthesia, and surrounded by a team of young and skilled surgeons, parents can't help but imagine every possible scenario that could happen. Many "what ifs" start to occupy their minds. It's one of the few moments in life when one feels genuinely helpless and may feel compelled to surrender to a force beyond control. The only option left is to trust in science and the experts, hoping they will provide the answers and possibly help their little ones.

The doctors told us that Olivia's surgery could take up to 7 hours in length. Can you imagine yourself holding your breath and trying to remain calm and positive during a time full of trepidation? It's natural to want to retreat from the world, curl up, and cry with anger and despair when life takes an unexpected turn. Who could have predicted that our once beautiful and perfect princess, who brought us so much joy just three and a half years ago, would trigger a series of events that turned our lives upside down? It's as if the rug was pulled from under us, leaving us treading in a sea of grief and heartache that we could never have imagined enduring in such a short time. As we sat alongside Mark's parents, we spent most of our time trying to keep busy, which meant doing what we do best, making small talk with other families. We hoped conversing with others would offer us hope and comfort, knowing that we were not alone. Some parents had children doing minor surgeries like appendix and tonsil removals, while only a handful had more complex procedures. Unfortunately, as we worked the room and learned more about each family's struggles, Olivia's surgery took home the most complicated and risky prize. Not something I was proud of that day by any means. I would have traded spots with any one of those parents if I could. Seated in those cold, blue leatherette chairs, each with its own mini table housing a box of tissues, we were left with nothing but time. Time to reflect. Time to think about how life would have been different if Olivia had not been diagnosed with TS. Time to think about her new life without seizures should the surgery be successful. We sat and sat and sat, and all we could do was wait. We were watching others wait. Some families were fortunate to be in the presence of their family and friends, supporting them with an abundance of food and positive encouragement. While others quietly sat in solitude, keeping themselves busy by reading or playing games on their phone. However, it seemed there was a common thread that weaved us all together, our unwavering love for our child and anticipation in our hearts that the surgery would provide them with the optimal results we were hoping for. *We all shared that same hope that day, alongside heartache and uncertainty. Pain and suffering don't discriminate. For once, I didn't feel alone. I felt like I belonged.*

I prayed this was just a blip in Olivia's long and healthy life. That we could leave behind this bad dream here in this cold, sterile space full of concrete floors and worn-out blue couches. How can one place hold so many mixed emotions? A place that has so much pain and sorrow for so many families yet so many aspirations and dreams for others.

Over time, we observed new families arrive in anguish while others leave in relief to meet up with their loved ones. It was pretty unnerving to see surgeons arrive in their blue smocks looking for their young patients' parents to discuss the surgery's status or to explain the results. No matter the situation, it's never an easy moment to digest. When we saw our surgeons enter the waiting room, our nerves were running on overdrive, and we pulled ourselves together to meet them in the discussion room to discuss Olivia's surgery. The room resembled a small board room. Two surgeons sat before us, reassuring us that the surgery was going well. They continued to explain that the resection posing a risk to her left-hand mobility was unnecessary. Upon resecting her right temporal lobe, they felt confident they had a good handle on the seizures. There was no need to resect further. It was an instant victory for Mark and me, yet we were still not out of the woodwork. We were relieved that Olivia would not have to take on yet another hurdle in her life, like a physical disability—a small lifeline amidst a tsunami.

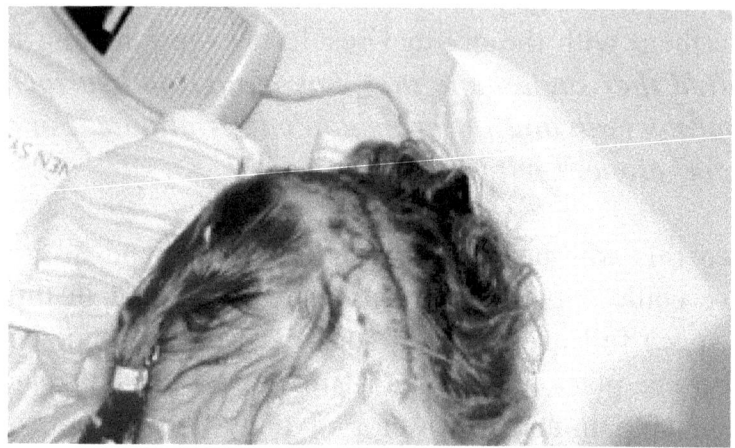

The incision post right temporal lobectomy surgery

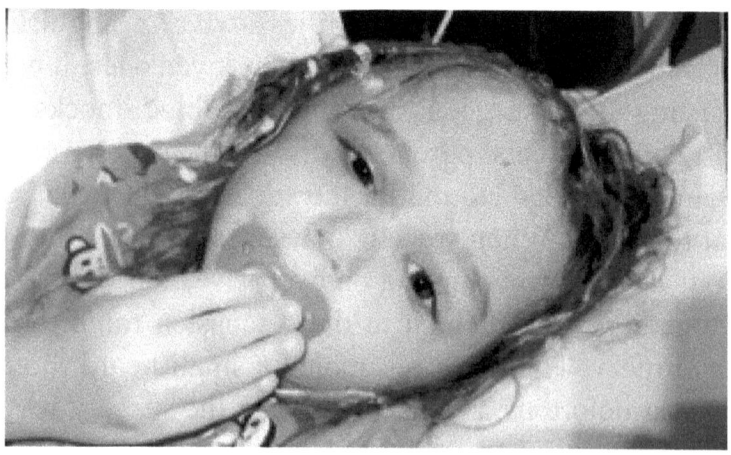

Olivia just an hour after brain surgery

A FRESH START

After a long night lying alongside Olivia in the ICU and watching her be monitored by nurses every hour, I was beyond exhausted. However, the terrific news that her surgery was a great success gave me instant hope, optimism and adrenaline which was my fuel to keep on going. Despite the fatigue, I was on an internal high, and I couldn't wait for her to open her big brown eyes and see me smiling and waiting for her with her favourite pink monkey.

Thanks to the nearby hotel we had booked days before, Mark and I took turns monitoring Olivia while the other could catch up on some much-needed rest, a hot shower and a chance to regroup our thoughts. We had been operating on overdrive for almost a week now, and we couldn't wait to get back to life as we knew it or maybe to something better.

After waking up in the ICU and passing all her vitals, she was transferred to a room for recovery. At this time, Olivia started to join us back in our world by opening her beautiful eyes and moving her arms and legs around. She began to smile when she saw my face, and I knew at that moment she was back. I was shocked and overjoyed when I heard her scream, "Potty." I couldn't believe she remembered the word and how to use it in context. So we pulled out her little portable potty, put it on the bed, and gently propped her up on it. Much to my surprise, I hear the lovely sound of urine entering the potty seat. I can't even begin to explain the exhilaration at that moment. Almost as though we had won the lottery!

Despite Olivia's grogginess and the dark and swollen eyes that resulted from her brain being exposed for lengthy periods, she had mini breakthroughs of laughter and smiles. It was reassuring to see that Olivia quickly felt better as the day went on. By the next day, Olivia sat upright in bed, singing and playing with her toys. No one could believe she had just undergone such an extensive surgery. She was the ray of sunshine **shining through** a slew of dark clouds. She was bright-eyed and cheerful.

After spending ten long days in the hospital, we were finally given the green light to go home. Even though we were thrilled to leave and return to a familiar place, we couldn't shake off the feeling of fear. The doctors reassured us that Olivia was progressing faster than expected, and not witnessing any seizures was an encouraging sign. This may have marked the true beginning of a new, better, and brighter life for Olivia.

BITTERSWEET HOMECOMING

Home never seemed sweeter. Our house appeared more inviting than my memory served, larger and quieter than I recalled. The joy of finally returning home to a place so full of familiarity, comfort and warmth. That intangible essence is what truly makes a house feel like a home. It wasn't the inanimate objects within it but the liberating sensation of belonging and freedom. Freedom from the constant checks by nurses and physicians every hour, from the disruptive sounds of bells and alarms due to equipment malfunctions, from the constant poking and prodding for various procedures, and from the echoing cries of children reluctant to cooperate or yearning for their parents. Being home was a cherished gift, a respite that felt like love hugging us from every corner. The mini messes that were left behind, did not even seem to phase me, as they usually would.

Yet, an unsettling feeling lingered within me, a constant juggling act of contrasting emotions. Guilt and gratitude vied for dominance once again, creating a tumultuous turmoil in my mind. I couldn't discern a clear emotional path as my thoughts seemed entangled.

Gratitude overwhelmed me for the successful surgery that brought my baby home, and I felt indebted to the benevolent forces above. However, the haunting realization of what I left behind in the hospital gnawed at me. My mind dwelled on the parents who were still awaiting surgeries for their children, their uncertainty about the outcomes mirroring my past anxieties. I envisioned them, weary and uncomfortable, sitting on those blue cold, emotionless chairs.

I couldn't shake the thoughts of those families I encountered in the ICU, facing grave situations. Some had been there for weeks, clinging to the dwindling hope of improvement for their children and a chance to leave the hospital. The image of pain and sorrow in their eyes remained branded in my mind as they sat beside their children, drained and helpless.

How much pain can a parent endure before they break? How unfair was it that I got a green card to escape the torment of the ICU, but they continued to stay with no end in sight? What can I possibly say to those parents that would comfort them or make them feel better? I couldn't put an end to these feelings of guilt. They continued to torment me day after day. Why couldn't I just feel blessed that I was lucky enough to have fate on our side? I found myself overwhelmed with trying to feel gratitude for simply being born in an extraordinary first-world country, where top-tier healthcare and a world-renowned children's hospital were just at my fingertips. The expertise of highly qualified physicians offered us the chance to enhance Olivia's life—a prospect that would have been unimaginable and unattainable in many parts of the world. Why couldn't I just be happy and grateful??

There was a complexity to my emotions. I believe it stems from the profound connections forged with the beautiful families I encountered during our hospital journey, connections that I will forever hold dear. We all navigated through a dark chapter in our lives together, where our children's health took precedence over everything else. In that shared experience, nothing else mattered except the sincere desire to return home with our children. Rose and Lauren, Jane and Jade, Kirra and Max, you will forever be in my heart, and I hope that one day we can meet again in a better place and life. A life that is fair and just. I dedicate this book to you all. The journey, the struggle, the pain, the rejection, and most of all, the unconditional love that makes parenting all that more challenging. If only we could break away, stop feeling, stop thinking, and stop hurting, then we could rise above and supersede our emotions. **_Humans are bound to experience pain and heartache in various forms, contributing to our personal growth. Life's hardships and experiences shape us into the individuals we are today. The more challenges we face, the more we become grounded and desensitized to the world around us, seeing it through a protected lens. Pain teaches us to be more resilient and adaptable to change, not only for our loved ones but also for ourselves. It's a valuable lesson that helps us survive and thrive in this unpredictable world._**

SHATTERED HOPES

After weeks of post-surgery recovery, it felt like we had been given a new lease on life. Olivia was completely back to her happy and joyful self and resumed pre-school without a hitch. It was heartwarming to see her flourishing in every way possible, from being more alert to singing and dancing at every chance she got. She became our little ray of sunshine after the storm, and we started seeing the world anew through her innocent eyes. Life was simply beautiful, and we cherished every moment of it.

A month following the surgery, our worst nightmare came true. Olivia had her first post-surgery seizure, which left us devastated and disheartened. The doctors warned us that seizures following surgery were not uncommon, but their persistence and similarity to her pre-surgery seizures were concerning. We immediately contacted our neurosurgeon, who provided us with grim feedback. He explained that the faulty wiring in Olivia's brain had been present since birth, and while the main culprit had been removed, other hidden areas could still cause seizures. The risk we took was significant. Although we hoped for a favourable outcome, the return of seizures indicated that different brain areas had been triggered, making future outbreaks likely. The surgeon delivered unexpected news regarding Olivia's brain pathology, shattering our previous understanding of her condition. Contrary to the initial diagnosis of Tuberous Sclerosis, her brain revealed non-cancerous lesions that had formed since birth. These lesions, deeply embedded within her brain tissue, posed a threat to its functionality, leading to unpredictable seizures. The revelation left us speechless, grappling with results we were unprepared to comprehend amidst the physical and emotional aftermath of the surgery.

I cannot decide what was more devastating, witnessing Olivia undergo surgery and recovery or receiving the bleak news that this might be a life-long sentence for her and us, with an unpredictable future. I felt utterly broken and defeated. It was truly the lowest point in my life. The realization that Olivia might have to suffer from seizures for the rest of her life was unbearable. How can we accept a life filled with endless medication, therapy sessions, and uncertainties? The weight of the situation was suffocating me, and my hope and faith, which had always sustained me, were slipping away! I couldn't comprehend why this was happening to us. ***Being helpless and unable to control our circumstances was too much to bear. I was spiralling down a path of self-blame and condemnation. "It was a dark and difficult time for me, and I knew I couldn't handle this alone. I needed help."***

EMBRACING THE LIFELINE

Several weeks had passed since we received the devastating news about Olivia's lifelong condition and the lack of effective seizure treatment. Despite my efforts to move forward, I felt stuck in a cycle of hopelessness and defeat. Days blurred together without any sense of purpose or motivation. The spark that once fueled my passion for life had faded away. Even the things I used to enjoy felt unbearable. I couldn't find joy in anything. It was as if a dark cloud had descended upon me, and I couldn't shake it off. I felt trapped in my own misery and wished to escape this never-ending nightmare. Despite my love for Olivia and Julian, their beauty and joy were no longer enough to lift me up and propel me forward.

Mark had had enough of watching me indulge in self-pity day after day. He recognized that my emotional state was not improving, and that was when he took action by suggesting therapy. At first, I was hesitant to seek help, as I didn't fully realize how severe my condition was or how it was affecting others. However, I knew that something needed to change if he and my family were deeply concerned. The thought of conversing with a professional offered a glimmer of hope, suggesting a path toward healing. Despite being unsure how to shift my perspective, I remained open to any possibility that could alleviate the darkness I was experiencing. It felt like I was clinging to the case of a miracle.

The day finally arrived for my appointment with the therapist. I was eager and hopeful. I was exhausted from feeling crippled by sadness and ungratefulness. My unhappiness consumed me to the point where I could not see beyond it. I needed someone to pull me out of this dark hole and guide me in recognizing the blessings in my life that I had forgotten about.

During my session with the therapist, I received some valuable insights about why I was feeling the way I was. The therapist offered reassurance, normalizing my feelings of anger and betrayal in response to Olivia's condition. She compared my experience to grieving, a lifelong process in my case. Encouraging me to be patient with myself, she highlighted my unique strengths that had contributed to Olivia's progress. Her words instilled a sense of empowerment, reminding me that Olivia was in capable hands, guided by someone who tirelessly advocated for her. She emphasized the importance of viewing life as a journey, not a destination, where facing challenges shapes our character. Although it can be challenging, having the knowledge that I have done everything within my control to ensure Olivia's well-being should give me the self-assurance and confidence needed to cope with the difficulties of co-existing with her condition. The confidence will help me rise above and move forward. This idea of acceptance struck a chord with me. I realized that I needed to come to terms with what I couldn't change and accept that life doesn't always go according to plan. It meant deviating from the path I had envisioned for myself but still striving to live the best life possible. It was a tough pill to swallow but a necessary one. When I left the therapist's office, I felt more optimistic than I had in a long time. *I was fully aware that learning to live with uncertainty and the unknown would be an ongoing challenge, however, I was determined to confront it with all my strength. Even if that was one of the only things I needed to do. I had no other option but to face it head-on. It felt like relinquishing control and allowing life to take the driver's seat while I reluctantly sat in the back, unsure of what journey lay ahead.*

FINDING SOLACE IN NATURE

Over the years, we gradually adapted to our new life of living with a child with special needs. Mark and I became experts at managing our family with Olivia and Julian, and we established a new routine that worked for us. Although Olivia's developmental progress was slower than expected, she was still progressing, thanks to specialized programs like ABA therapy and occupational and physical therapy. However, her daily seizures were a constant struggle that I was determined to conquer. It became my newest hobby. Our days were filled with school, treatments, therapy sessions and supporting Julian's athletic pursuits in the evenings and on weekends. Watching Julian excel in sports gave me a much-needed break from the stresses of caring for Olivia and the motivation to face each day with renewed strength.

Living on the country property with 10 acres of land surrounding us was the perfect place for us at that time. Olivia could enjoy the open fields and the freedom to roam around. Her hammock was her favourite spot, where we spent many days gazing at the sky and singing "Twinkle Twinkle." Other times, we would find her covered in sand, laughing hysterically while sitting in her sandbox. The beauty of nature and the presence of living things helped Olivia flourish and **shine through**, and most importantly, it helped us deal with our difficult circumstances.

We found solace in taking tranquil strolls along the wooden bridge that arched over the sprawling pond. The soothing trickle of the nearby waterfall cascading down the ravine and into a bed of rocks provided a serene background melody to our nature walks. The fountain, with its swishing sound as it shot up into the sky, was a favourite place of ours while it provided the most perfect backdrop for all of our family photos. We marvelled at the graceful flow of the river as if it were imparting a lesson to us about surrendering and embracing freedom. It was nature that was teaching us how to live and survive amidst challenging times. It allowed me to shift my focus from the things I couldn't control and enjoy life's simple beauties surrounding us. In the spring, we would eagerly observe the geese as they crossed the grassy hills with their little ones in tow on their way to the river. Perched high above the house, we always had the company of crows, who seemed to watch over us like guardian angels. We never felt alone. We felt like we belonged.

Julian also found serenity in the country. He would spend every free moment exploring the trails on his dirt bike with his cousins and building forts in the forest, allowing his creativity to flow. Witnessing him thrive and relish life as any other child filled me with profound joy. He deserved every moment of happiness, and the countryside provided the ideal setting.

The countryside was a little paradise that gave us exactly what we needed. It was our daily mental escape from the stresses of the critical world. We found peace in the natural beauty of the environment and living things, which had a healing effect on us all from the inside out.

Olivia happy and peaceful on our country property

GOD MUST HATE YOU

As the school year approached, Julian, Olivia, and I braved the bustling crowds at Square One shopping mall in Mississauga, in search of new backpacks and shoes, a tradition we always did together. However, what should have been a joyful outing turned into a moment that will forever be engraved in my memory. Eventually, we arrived at our go-to store for school shoes, GEOX. We always loved their colourful selection and could count on their durability to last the whole year with minimal wear and tear.

As soon as we entered the store, Julian eagerly darted around the displays, selecting styles and colors he liked. Meanwhile, Olivia and I settled on a bench, waiting for the sales assistant to retrieve Julian's sizes. Restlessness took hold of Olivia, prompting her to rise from the bench. She started walking toward the shelves, pulling numerous shoes off and tossing them onto the ground, all the while babbling incoherently and smiling. Julian, feeling embarrassed, quickly rushed over and scooped her up, bringing her over to me. The look on his face conveyed his mortification, and he announced he didn't want to shop anymore, storming out of the store. Though I tried to call him back, he was already seated on a bench in the mall's main hallway. Apologizing to the sales assistant, Olivia and I exited the store. I promised to return later but unfortunately never did.

As I sat down beside Julian, I asked why he became so upset and left the store. He shared his frustration, finding Olivia's behaviour embarrassing and questioning why she had to act that way. Then, to my surprise, he dropped an unforeseen bombshell and asked me, "God must hate you, Mom?" Taken aback, I recognized that this moment had been looming, requiring a quick and thoughtful response. After taking a deep breath and seeking guidance from within, I explained to Julian in the best way I knew how.

I started by acknowledging the validity of his question, confirming that it was something I had questioned myself many times before. I understood that he might have felt that way, just as I had in the past. However, I went on to explain that over the years, I had come to realize that Olivia was meant to be an integral part of our family. She chose us as her parents and him as her brother. God must have had a plan in place, knowing we were equipped to handle the challenges of caring for a child as complex as Olivia. While other families might have struggled even more with a child like her, God knew that we had the time, resources, and patience to invest in her well-being. I reassured Julian that Olivia was fortunate to have him in her life, bringing her immense joy in various ways. In essence, I conveyed that God doesn't hate us; it's quite the opposite. As I met Julian's gaze, I could see the weight of his question hanging in the air between us. "Do I have to take care of Olivia when you are gone?" he asked, his voice barely above a whisper. It was a powerful question, one that I wasn't quite prepared for, but I knew that this was the perfect moment to address all of his concerns. Julian had always been a boy of few words, and when he did speak, it was because he had something very important to say. I took a deep breath, trying to gather my thoughts before answering his question. I explained to Julian that while Olivia is his sister, it is not his obligation to be her caregiver in the future. However, as her brother, it is his responsibility to consider what is best for her and her overall health and happiness. I went on to say that any future decisions about Olivia's care would be made as a family, with everyone's input considered. Our top priority will always be prioritizing Olivia's needs and determining what is best for her. Over time, we will continue to learn how to make these decisions. As I glanced at Julian's expression, it seemed as though a giant weight had been lifted off his shoulders, and he instantly felt better. He then said "OK, can we get popcorn now?" and just like that the topic was dropped and life went on as normal. As though the conversation never even happened.

I consider myself incredibly fortunate that as a child, Julian never complained, despite being the sibling of a special needs child. Maybe it was his innate personality or the experiences he had gone through, but Julian was precisely the child we needed to manage the pressures and stress of our complex life. He had developed the unique qualities of patience, compassion, self-sufficiency, and an ability to not demand, which made him a perfect fit for our family's circumstances. He was a true gift from God, a hidden gem that added immeasurable value to our lives. ***Our children are our greatest teachers; every experience with them helps us grow as parents. We learn from them and become better equipped to handle whatever life throws our way.***

EXPANDING OUR HEARTS

For years, I've grappled with a significant question: should we have more children? It's been a constant internal struggle, with days where I felt overwhelmed, leading me to dismiss the idea entirely, while on brighter days, the desire to expand our family consumed my thoughts.

I had always dreamt of having a big family, as both Mark and I came from families with two siblings. Life just didn't feel complete for me after having Olivia. It felt as though there was a large void in my family, however amid difficult moments, I frequently pondered, "How would I have handled this if I had a newborn or a toddler in tow?"

As the years went by, I used to daydream often about being pregnant or bringing home a newborn into our family and wondering what that would look like or how the kids would react. I was confident Julian would be thrilled to have someone to enjoy his adventures with, but would Olivia really care? I would often find myself projecting into the future, imagining my son navigating life with a sense of loneliness without experiencing the bond of having a typical sibling relationship like Mark and I had. It saddened me deeply. Whenever Julian visited his cousins' houses and witnessed their close interactions, he would return home with a sense of sadness. I remember him including a heartfelt plea for more siblings in his night prayers, which broke my heart. Despite his immense love and care for Olivia, it was clear that she didn't entirely reciprocate the depth of affection. Olivia often seemed absorbed in her own world, showing little interest in her surroundings, even when Julian was around. Her behaviour was unpredictable, and her interests differed greatly from those of a typical child. I found myself puzzled by this dynamic. While I understood that Julian and Olivia were learning from each other uniquely, I didn't want Julian to miss out on the experience of having neurotypical siblings as he grew up. Mark and I cherish the memories we created with our siblings during our upbringing. Our family activities and shared interests played a significant role in shaping our lives and bringing us joy. I always celebrated my brother's accomplishments, whether it was cheering on Nico at his hockey games, where he consistently earned the MVP award or supporting Rocky in his school fashion shows. The bond we shared as siblings holds a special place in my heart. I often reminisce about our long Sunday brunches, where we would spend countless hours engaged in deep conversations over a delicious home-cooked meal. Or the fact that Mark still had another sibling to experience life with, even after losing his brother, makes me wonder how things would have been if it had only been the two of them. Those cherished moments have stayed with us well into adulthood, shaping our upbringing and identity and grounding us amidst life's twists and turns. It's only natural to desire the same for Julian. I want him to experience the joys of growing up alongside a sibling, forging a bond that can withstand any challenge and bring endless love and understanding into his life.

I know Olivia will always provide him happiness in her own unique way, but how can Julian navigate through life without a sibling to lean on in our absence or help make decisions regarding her well-being? The internal debate was pressing on me and only growing as time went on.

During Christmas 2011, the longing to grow our family became even more pronounced. Although I was immensely grateful for my two children, there was an undeniable sense of incompleteness, as if someone was missing from our family portrait. I couldn't help but notice the empty space between Julian and Olivia in our Christmas cards. Every outing with them was accompanied by an imagined scenario of me juggling a baby in a car seat carrier while securely holding onto Olivia's hand. Thoughts of how I would manage with another baby in the mix consistently occupied my mind as if I were mentally preparing for an eventuality. At bedtime, as I read them stories and kissed them goodnight, my gaze would often wander towards the empty guest room, where I would envision another child joining our loving household. This yearning grew stronger over time, refusing to fade away.

Whenever I brought up the idea of expanding our family, Mark would quickly dismiss it with comments like, "You're crazy" or "Why would you want to complicate our lives even more?" It was disheartening to feel that he couldn't understand the emptiness and longing I was experiencing. While he found contentment in our current family dynamic, spending quality time with Julian through activities like minor league baseball, I was left to care for Olivia at home. Whether managing her therapy sessions or handling her seizures, the responsibility always fell on my shoulders. There were times when I couldn't help but feel a sense of resentment, as this wasn't the life I had envisioned for myself. Regret, disappointment, and the feeling of missing out on significant milestones became a constant presence in my thoughts and emotions. My future would be a solitary journey focused solely on meeting Olivia's needs.

While Mark enjoyed and celebrated the milestones and achievements with Julian effortlessly, I couldn't help but feel a mix of envy and sadness. It was difficult to genuinely share in their experiences when I knew all too well what I was missing out on. The path I embarked on with Olivia took me on a different trajectory than Mark's, and I couldn't shake the longing for what could have been. Being Olivia's primary caregiver meant shouldering the responsibilities and challenges that came with it. Navigating through life tackling one hurdle at a time. I guess deep down, I wished for a simpler path, one where I could revel in the same sense of happiness and accomplishment that Mark felt. I recognized that our situation was unique, and merely swapping roles with Mark wasn't feasible. His dedication to providing for our family and covering Olivia's medical expenses demanded his full attention at work. While he couldn't be as involved in Olivia's day-to-day routines, he actively participated in decision-making and shared my frustrations. His unwavering support gave me a sense of balance and stability during times when it was volatile and necessary. Mark and I embraced different roles within our family, each contributing in our own way. Despite the difficulties, we understood that staying committed to our respective roles and responsibilities was crucial for our happiness and survival. Despite the hurdles posed by Olivia's condition, we remained a united team, always supporting each other.

The thoughts of extending our family continued to fuel my determination to have a sincere and open conversation with Mark, emphasizing the significance and gravity of the decision we were facing. Before it was too late, he needed to understand the depth of my feelings and the potential impact on our family dynamics.

In January 2012, on a Monday afternoon, our children happily engaged in play in the background. I managed to persuade Mark to engage in a serious discussion about the potential of expanding our family. Surprisingly, he agreed to listen attentively. Mark proposed that we each compile a list of the pros and cons of this decision, scheduling a follow-up meeting on Friday to share our findings. This response encapsulated Mark's character perfectly—always calculated and rational. Given his methodical and logical nature, it seemed as if he approached this decision as a business matter. I wholeheartedly embraced this approach as someone who thrived on organization and lists. Utilizing my vast experience in sales, I eagerly took on the challenge of crafting a compelling proposal to win over Mr. Skeptic.

Throughout that week, I poured my heart and soul into creating a comprehensive list that captured all aspects of our family dynamics and potential outcomes should we decide to have another child. Here is how our lists unfolded:

LIANA'S LIST

PROS:

- Providing Julian with a lifelong companion and sibling to share experiences with

- Having another family member actively participates in Olivia's medical decisions

- Utilizing the available space in our large house, which currently has empty bedrooms

- Having the financial means to support another child
- Having a live-in nanny already in place to assist with childcare
- Being currently unemployed, allowing for more time and flexibility
- Enjoying the experience of pregnancy without any previous complications
- Benefiting from extensive support from both sides of the family
- Sharing a common mindset of being driven, organized, and logical
- Minimizing the impact on my husband's life, as there would be no additional demands on his part

CONS:

- The slight possibility of having another child with special needs
- Adding more responsibilities and tasks to an already full schedule
- Potentially needing to purchase a larger vehicle to accommodate the expanded family
- Incurring additional expenses for future travel, such as requiring a second hotel room
- Being cranky and miserable for the rest of my life if we don't expand our family

MARK'S LIST:

PROS:

- None

CONS:

- A chance that the child may have special needs
- More expensive
- More headaches /stress
- More time involved with the newborn will take away from Olivia's care
- Julian will be forgotten

Friday arrived sooner than anticipated, and I was fully prepared to state my case. Determined with conviction, I went first in presenting my list to Mark at the breakfast bar. I carefully addressed each point, explaining my reasoning and emphasizing the long-term implications of our decision. I concluded by expressing my fears of growing resentful and unfulfilled if we didn't seize this opportunity. "Would you want to live with a cranky and angry old woman in your older years?" I would say to him as I concluded, as though that point alone was going to win him over. I wanted him to understand the magnitude of my emotions and the potential impact on our future. I was prepared to fight for what I strongly believed in. Mark's response was unexpected, as he listened attentively and eventually raised his arms in surrender, saying a simple "OK." I couldn't discern if he was genuinely convinced or chose to yield to avoid a potentially greater conflict in the future. Nonetheless, a sense of relief washed over me as we finally agreed. This incident showed Mark's character and his willingness to compromise and prioritize our collective well-being. He possessed strength and determination, much like myself, but he also demonstrated immense respect and trust in me and my feelings. His compassionate nature and unwavering belief in me, especially when it came to Olivia's care, was something I cherished deeply about Mark. He placed his complete confidence in me, never doubting my abilities or decisions. It was a truly wonderful feeling to be so supported and believed in by someone I loved. He explained that he didn't want me to be unhappy in the future, and if expanding our family was the key to my happiness, he was entirely on board. It felt like a significant weight was lifted off of me to have his support. We decided to try that very night, and much to our surprise, just three weeks later, we discovered that #3 was on the way.

MY SISTER'S KEEPER

In 2013, we welcomed the birth of our third child, Lauren, on January 6. Her arrival at the beginning of the year seemed symbolic of her place in the world. She was the leader that we would soon learn to know. She felt like a true blessing, sent to us from the heavens above. She was eager to embrace the new year and had something great to offer our family. She was the child I had dreamt about, envisioned, and, most importantly, needed. The timing couldn't have been more perfect, as if a higher power orchestrated it. Thank you, Allan! With her arrival, my faith and beliefs started to be restored, and I couldn't ignore the signs that had been present throughout the years. It became clear then that there was a reason for my restlessness and void. I now realized those signs were essential for her existence, guiding us toward something extraordinary. Lauren's presence in our family felt destined as if she had chosen us to be her parents. It seemed she had a significant role to play and much to contribute. She was on a mission, and her life's purpose was yet to be discovered.

Bringing our beautiful baby girl home was a joyous moment. Lauren, weighing a whopping 8.3 lbs, had captivating big blue eyes and a head full of thick black locks. She, indeed, was a sight to behold. She exuded contentment and ease from the beginning, making our days brighter and more manageable. Lauren became our ray of sunshine during those cloudy dark days, which was precisely what we needed. She was a delightful distraction during challenging times that I was longing for. Her presence in our lives brought simplicity, pure joy, and a much-needed respite from the complexities of life. Caring for Lauren felt comparatively easier compared to the daily struggles of parenting a child with seizures and delays. She brought a sense of lightness and happiness that lifted our spirits.

As the months drew closer to the six-month milestone, my anxiety grew, and I closely monitored every little movement Lauren made. The memory of witnessing Olivia's seizures during that same period undoubtedly haunted me, and the mere thought of having to endure such a nightmare again with another child was unbearable. I didn't want to subject Lauren to unnecessary tests and screenings at such a tender age unless apparent symptoms presented themselves. And so, day after day, I remained vigilant, observing her every move, ensuring that each action was expected and free from any signs of distress. Silently harbouring a deep-seated fear, I kept that secret tucked away within me that I had never shared with anyone.

She not only exceeded our expectations but having a neurotypical child like Lauren at such a young age made me realize what I had been missing. Parenting became easier, and watching her effortlessly reach her milestones brought me joy. It was a much-needed mental break from focusing solely on Olivia's challenges. After dedicating seven years to supporting Olivia with minimal progress, I found that with Lauren, I could redirect my energy and in turn, simply appreciate Olivia for who she was. It was a hard but necessary lesson. It was important for Olivia to feel loved and accepted without sensing my stress or often disappointment. Olivia was always in tune with the energies of others and having Lauren as a positive presence in our family helped create a stronger bond. *Lauren became the glue that brought us all together and Julian's much-needed sibling. Together we were now a complete family.*

As Lauren grew, we began to see little signs of compassion towards Olivia at such an early age. Lauren would often sit beside Olivia in her high chair and hold her hand while calling her by her nickname "NANI", which meant sleep. A name that was given by Julian when he was very young. Olivia often slept after having seizures so it was quite fitting for the time. It stuck like glue and extended family all began to call her that over time. Lauren was becoming interested in Olivia's behaviour and quirks and would often mimic her. It was quite comical at that time, seeing Olivia repeating her favorite word of the day which she often did and then Lauren repeating the same word. It felt like I had two toddlers in unison, which is probably why they got along so well.

When it came to potty training, I decided to tackle the challenge with both Olivia and Lauren simultaneously. Despite Olivia's prior progress, setbacks from seizures and surgery hindered her development in this area. However, Lauren surprised us with her quick learning and cooperation, smoothing the process. Having a child who eagerly participated and picked up new skills effortlessly was bittersweet. Lauren even took the initiative to assist Olivia, guiding her to the toilet while using a nearby portable potty herself. While Lauren excelled in potty training, Olivia continued to struggle due to the disconnect between her brain and body, making it difficult for her to master this skill.

Despite the challenges of having two toddlers, Lauren naturally found ways to assist me with Olivia, even without realizing it, especially during challenging moments. She possessed a sense of calmness and reassurance that provided great comfort. Every skill that Lauren acquired, she felt compelled to help Olivia develop as well. There were instances when Lauren would sit in her highchair and assist Olivia with her meals. She would carefully pick up any fallen morsels or crumbs and attempt to hand-feed Olivia, who always welcomed her gestures. In other moments, while enjoying the tranquillity of our countryside property, we would observe Julian riding his small dirt bike around the house. Olivia would as usual flutter about the driveway, gazing up at the sky with a wide smile, humming her favourite tune. She appeared like a graceful butterfly soaring above us, utterly oblivious to the world around her. Lauren had a keen sense of awareness and a deep bond with Olivia. She would quickly rush over to hold Olivia's hand, ensuring her safety, especially when her brother made his turn around the house. Lauren's protective instincts kicked in, as she didn't want Olivia to be accidentally run over. Lauren's natural instinct to assist and protect Olivia was genuinely heartwarming. She possesses a unique awareness of Olivia's needs and went above and beyond to provide support, even at such a young age. It was as if she understood her sister's vulnerabilities and took it upon herself to be her guardian. Indeed, Lauren's actions exemplify being *"**my sister's keeper.**"* Her unwavering devotion to Olivia was undeniable, bringing immeasurable happiness to our family. Witnessing their bond and the deep love they shared filled our hearts with warmth. In those moments, it was evident that their connection went beyond the typical sibling relationship. *Lauren's innate understanding of Olivia's needs and her willingness to support and protect her showcased a level of compassion and empathy that was truly remarkable. As parents, we couldn't have asked for a more beautiful example of sisterly love, and it enriched our lives in ways we couldn't have anticipated.*

Lauren at age 3

SEIZE THE OPPORTUNITY

On August 8, 2013, as I scrolled through social media in an attempt to divert my mind from negative thoughts swirling through my mind, a news story immediately seized my attention. It was a documentary by Dr. Sanjay Gupta, a CNN medical correspondent, titled "WEED." The report highlighted a story about the FIGI family residing in Colorado. The family consisted of three children: a boy around Julian's age, approximately nine years old, and twin girls around Olivia's age, about seven years old.

The story focuses on one of the twin girls named Charlotte, who began experiencing seizures at the tender age of two. Eventually, she was diagnosed with Dravet Syndrome, an extremely severe form of epilepsy in infancy. Charlotte's seizures were debilitating, with episodes occurring as frequently as 300 grand mal seizures per week. As a result, she lost all her developmental skills since the diagnosis, and her prognosis seemed bleak.

Driven by desperation, Charlotte's mother Paige, approached the Stanley Family, who owned a cannabis farm in Colorado Springs, hoping to find a solution for her daughter. The family, empathetic to her situation, offered her an oil derived from a marijuana plant known as "Hippies Disappointment," which had a low THC content and high CBD levels. Although they had no personal use for it, they held onto a glimmer of hope that it could help Charlotte.

The results were nothing short of extraordinary. With this CBD oil, Charlotte experienced an immediate reduction in her epileptic seizures, going from 300 per week to just two or three per month. The impact of her story reverberated across North

America, gaining widespread media attention and instilling hope in families with similar diagnoses or symptoms of intractable seizures. However, there was a caveat: for children to receive this treatment, they had to reside in Colorado Springs, where the oil was available for purchase.

As I read the article, I became electrified and empowered by its possibilities. Without hesitation, I rushed over to my husband, who was diligently working on his computer. Bursting with excitement, I struggled to put my words together as I shared the link with him. Together, we watched the documentary on his desktop computer, our faces filled with excitement, uncertainty, and fear.

As we looked at each other, the weight of Olivia's daily seizures and the ineffectiveness of her current pharmaceutical regime weighed heavy on our hearts. Could this newfound possibility provide hope for Olivia and potentially change her life? The thought lingered in our minds as we sat there, weighing out all of our options. At this point in Olivia's life, I was feeling demoralized and drained. I had spent so much time, money and resources since her diagnosis to improve her quality of life, only to be disappointed time and time again. It became clear to us that if we didn't seize this opportunity, we may be forced to live in regret for years to come. Could this be the missing piece to Olivia's life puzzle that we have been long waiting for? Witnessing Olivia's daily seizures and the toll it took on her fragile little body was heart-wrenching. The chance of any type of seizure reduction and possibly an improved life was worth all the gamble. With a deep understanding that our purpose as parents to Olivia was to exhaust every avenue, we devised a plan. Olivia's health was always our top priority, and we couldn't stand idle by the darkness and confusion that had taken hold of her tender little brain anymore. Fueled by unwavering hope in our hearts and without a moment's hesitation, we embarked on the next chapter of our lives, venturing south of the border with our entire family in tow.

Despite the challenges of juggling the needs of Julian at age 10, Olivia at age 8, and baby Lauren at almost 1, our unwavering devotion to Olivia's well-being became our driving force. As a family, we had to embrace this journey together in the name of unconditional love. After all, that's what families do!

THE UNEXPECTED DETOUR

In the months leading up to our relocation to the United States, we faced numerous challenges. One of the main hurdles was finding suitable accommodations that could accommodate our growing family while catering to Olivia's unique medical needs. Additionally, we had to navigate through the complex and bureaucratic process of paperwork and documentation required to access the treatment she needed in the new country.

This process began by obtaining numerous letters from physicians in Canada stating that the cannabis treatment was unavailable locally. After multiple visits with our Canadian border security agency and providing all the required documentation, we were finally granted a one-year extended travel visa for medical purposes. We were one step closer to an opportunity that could change Olivia's life forever.

Excited and fearful, we began to take the necessary steps to plan for this harrowing adventure. We decided to trade our SUV truck for an economical minivan. This choice allowed us to efficiently pack and transport all our personal possessions required for our extended stay, as we embarked on this life-changing journey across the country. The minivan provided our family with the necessary space and comfort, ensuring that we were well-prepared for the upcoming transition. We found a modest home to rent near the Figi family in Colorado Springs, that not only accommodated our family's needs but allowed us to be close to the local school that both for Julian and Olivia were enrolled. Throughout this period, we faced numerous obstacles, but our unwavering determination and commitment to Olivia's well-being propelled us forward. We were all in and ready to leave no stone unturned in our quest for a better future for our beloved daughter.

As our carefully laid plans seemed to fall into place, an unexpected and devastating event shattered our world. In November of 2013, Mark's heart decided to suddenly fail, casting a shadow of uncertainty over everything we had been working towards. It all began with pain in his left elbow the week before, which initially led to a green pass from the local hospital's emergency department. However, the pain soon escalated into extreme lethargy, weakness, and profuse sweating, prompting us to rush him back to the emergency room, this time by ambulance.

The paramedics wasted no time in assessing the gravity of the situation. Their swift evaluation confirmed that Mark was indeed having a heart attack. As those words were abruptly spoken, I was overcome with shock and disbelief. At that moment, my instincts kicked in, and I immediately went into "mama bear" mode, determined to shield my children from the unknown outcome that lay ahead. I can still vividly recall the image of little Julian, alongside his cousin Benjamin, their faces pressed through the iron pickets of the staircase, looking down to an array of paramedics filled with confusion and fear. They watched them swiftly carry Mark away on a stretcher through our double front doors. It's a sombre image that remains embossed in my memory. One I wish never existed!

Amid the devastation and fear, questions raced through my mind. Why, God? What lesson are we meant to learn from this? Our focus had always been on Olivia's well-being and our plans to seek alternative treatment. How could we move forward with this unexpected fork in the road?

The sudden events left us grappling with uncertainty and a profound sense of vulnerability. The immediate priority was Mark's health and recovery, unfortunately shifting our attention from Olivia's treatment. *As we navigated this new challenge, we clung to the hope that there was a greater purpose behind it all, even if we couldn't yet comprehend it. We would need to draw strength from one another and reach down to grasp the resilience within that had carried us through all our difficult times.*

COURAGE IN THE FACE OF CHANGE

After undergoing a crucial stent procedure, Mark was discharged from the hospital within a remarkably short period of 24 hours. It was quite daunting as we left the hospital with a concoction of medications and a whole new life plan. He returned home feeling fragile, weakened, and apprehensive about what lay ahead. His sudden heart-related episode perplexed us, as no pre-existing medical conditions could warrant it. As we contemplated the upcoming trip to Colorado, we couldn't help but ponder its potential influence in setting off this unforeseen event. It's possible that the sheer magnitude of his emotions and the stress stemming from our impending move, coupled with the enduring grief we faced with our daughter's condition, had finally reached a breaking point for him. Not to mention, the tragic passing of his brother on a motorcycle was never truly dealt with during that time. This accumulation of stressors might have struck a deep chord within his being.

As we confronted the reality of his condition, we knew that our journey to Colorado would have to now take a back seat, and consideration for Mark's well-being became first priority. We decided to put our moving plans on hold and shifted our focus towards supporting him during his recovery and ensuring that he had the necessary support systems as we embarked on this new chapter of our lives.

Overwhelmed by sadness, I couldn't help but feel a deep sense of fear and loneliness. The weight of responsibility now fell solely on my shoulders, and having to be strong for everyone, especially my partner, seemed intimidating. Where would I find the internal strength to carry on? It felt like I was being pushed to my maximum limits, facing this battle alone. But despite the overwhelming circumstances, I knew deep down that I had no choice but to rise above and be present for my family when they needed me the most. In this moment of uncertainty, I came to a profound realization: strength resides deep within each of us, waiting to be awakened and harnessed. We often overlook or underestimate the reserve of resilience and determination. Despite the challenges before me, I knew I possessed an inner wellspring of courage and tenacity, ready to be tapped into. I knew it was the confidence within me that was a result of all my parent's teachings that were now coming to fruition. I began to embrace the power within me that had been instilled for all these years. That deeply rooted foundation of assurance allowed me to believe in myself and refuse to succumb to despair. To persevere when faced with adversity. I began to understand that strength is not merely a physical attribute but also a mental and emotional force. I was the only one who held the key to unlocking this strength, and harnessing it was up to me. With a conscious decision, I mustered my courage and tackled this new hurdle that lay before me. I put on my metaphorical "big girl shorts" and decided to face the challenge head-on. "BRING IT ON BABY" became my new favourite motto, a powerful declaration of my determination to own and conquer my challenges.

A month later, Mark and I had a much-needed heartfelt conversation about our decision to move to Colorado. We recognized the importance of prioritizing Mark's recovery, but Olivia's daily seizures had become unbearable, and time was of the essence. It was an incredibly difficult choice, but after healthcare professionals advised Mark against flying for the next three months, he selflessly suggested that I proceed with our original plan to travel south of the border with the kids on January 1st. Meanwhile, he and his father would drive our belongings in the van a few days earlier.

His selflessness and concern for our family touched me deeply. Despite his own challenges, he wanted to ensure that the children and I could start our new life in Colorado without delay. This arrangement would allow him to focus on his recovery with the support of his parents and be in a better condition to support our family once we settled in Colorado. It was a testament to his love and commitment, always placing our needs above his own.

We proceeded to book a flight for January 1st, 2014 tp Colorado Springs, symbolizing a fresh start and new beginnings. The kids were enrolled in the local school, Edith Wolford, ready to begin their classes soon after our arrival. It felt like the perfect timing to embark on this new adventure while offering stability for our children's education and daily routines as we started our new life together.

As the departure date rapidly approached, emotions ran high, and the weight of the decision felt heavy and unbearable at times. However, we knew in our hearts it was the right choice for our family. We clung to the hope that this move would provide Olivia with the care and support she desperately needed. With mixed feelings of anticipation and sadness, we prepared ourselves for the journey ahead, knowing we were united in our determination to create a better future for our children. Although the road ahead would be challenging, we were resolute in facing it together, even if physically apart for a short while. Our love and commitment to each other and our children would guide us through this transition. We held onto the belief that our reunion in Colorado would be a joyous and celebratory moment.

The long-awaited day had finally come when Mark and his father were embarking on their own special journey together to Colorado. My heart overflowed with joy, witnessing their shared excitement for this adventure. Earlier that morning, we bid our own personal farewells, filled with a deep sense of satisfaction knowing that we each found a life partner who shared the same vision and commitment to our children. We were united in our purpose, willing to go to great lengths to ensure a brighter future for them. With our new van packed to the brim of personal belongings and anticipation coursing through our veins, I stood there waving as it made its way down the long country driveway. Waving goodbye, I clung to the hope that they would reach their destination safely and forge unforgettable bonds along the way.

A few days later, it was finally our turn to head to the airport and begin our own adventure to Colorado. It was a day filled with a whirlwind of emotions for me. I couldn't shake off the feeling of intimidation that seemed to grapple me. It was as if all the unexpected events that had unfolded in the past month had suddenly caught up with me that morning. Why did it have to happen now, I wondered? I knew I had to be strong for my family. I desperately needed to approach this journey with confidence and a sense of control. There was simply no room for self-pity, especially not today. Just when my mind began to spiral, my kids appeared in my room, bursting with excitement for the trip we had been eagerly anticipating. It was almost as if they sensed I needed a wake-up call from this negative mental state that was lurking. It seemed it was their innocent way of reminding me that there was no time to waste. We had a distinct plan to follow, and we had to keep propelling forward, just as we always did. Indeed, today was not the day to deviate from our path.

As we loaded up the airport limo with my parents, who had decided to join us following Mark's heart attack, a wave of sadness washed over me momentarily. I couldn't help but feel a tinge of melancholy for what we were leaving behind. The place that had once been our source of immense joy would now become a distant memory. The vibrant autumn colours lining the driveway, the geese gracefully flocking to the nearby pond in spring, the trees bursting with life during the summer, and the enchanting winter wonderland that transformed the landscape—every season had its unique beauty. Would our new home in Colorado offer us the same level of enchantment and love? As we drove away, I found myself gazing back at our property until it vanished from sight. It felt as if I was seeing it in a different light, knowing it would be a long while before I set eyes on it again. "Farewell, Caledon. Goodbye home. You were good to us. We will miss you".

NEW YEAR, NEW HOME, NEW HOPE

After settling into our new home in the beautiful Flying Horse subdivision of Colorado Springs, we eagerly began exploring the surrounding community. It didn't take us long for us to discover the local parks, engage in friendly conversations with our neighbours, and even take a tour of the elementary school our children would soon attend, Edith Wolford. To our surprise, the transition was much smoother than anticipated.

One of the reasons for this smooth adjustment was undoubtedly the breathtaking views surrounding us. The majestic mountains and the stunning landscapes painted a picturesque backdrop for our new life. Living in beautiful Colorado Springs felt like being in God's Country. We instantly felt connected to nature and found solace in its presence. The view from the back of the house, with the mountains reaching toward the sky and the warm glow of the sun reflecting off their peaks and valleys, created a sense of warmth, tranquillity and wonder. We were so honoured to call this beautiful place our new home.

But it wasn't just the scenery that captured our hearts. The weather in Colorado Springs was a delightful surprise, with its abundance of warm and sunny days. The constant presence of the sun seemed to infuse the community with a sense of cheerfulness and contentment. It didn't take long for us to discover that Colorado enjoys over 300 days of sunshine each year, which undoubtedly impacts the residents of the community in a positive way. Everyone always seemed so happy!!

After settling into our new home, I had the pleasure of meeting Heather Jackson, a remarkable woman from Realm of Caring who had been instrumental in making our journey to Colorado possible. She was the compassionate and supportive individual I had been communicating with back home, and meeting her in person filled me with gratitude and admiration.

During our conversation, we learned that we were the second Canadian family to embark on this medical marijuana journey, joining a community of over 200 families from across the United States who had uprooted their lives for the same purpose. The CNN story had gone viral, resonating with families worldwide. Heather's dedication and unwavering support played a pivotal role in making our transition to Colorado a reality. As a Canadian, it wasn't an easy process to become a temporary resident in Colorado, but Heather's determination and assistance defied all odds. I felt immensely grateful for her efforts and considered her our guiding light during this harrowing time. She was our hidden gem, our guardian angel during our time in Colorado Springs. Heather was a vital connection for us and had a personal stake in this journey, as her son Zach was also receiving the same treatment. Her firsthand experience made her an invaluable resource and a trusted contact person for all families settling into their new lives in Colorado.

Later that week, we had the incredible pleasure and opportunity to meet Paige Figi, the mother of Charlotte Figi, who had become an internet sensation and played a vital role in driving numerous families to Colorado. It was Charlotte's story, featured on CNN, that had sparked a movement and inspired families from far and wide to seek the same treatment for their children.

In the act of remarkable kindness, Paige organized a meet and greet event for all the families at her country property, nestled amidst the woods and conveniently located just down the road from our new home. As we gathered around a warm bonfire under the starlit sky, we had the privilege of meeting families who had travelled great distances, driven by a glimmer of hope and the sheer determination to find a solution for their child's lifelong condition. The Bureschi family, The Bogner family, and The Pogson family to name a few.

The atmosphere was filled with a palpable sense of camaraderie and shared experiences. Conversations flowed freely as parents openly exchanged stories, shared triumphs and challenges, and offered support and encouragement to one another.

We were all united with our special needs children around this golden flame which not only brought us together as one family, but for once since Olivia's diagnosis, I felt like I belonged. I couldn't explain it in words, but the overwhelming feeling of being accepted, understood and not judged for once within a group of strangers was remarkable. Each family present had their unique tale of resilience and unwavering love for their child, bound together by the common pursuit of a better quality of life with this new treatment that they called "Charlotte's Web", named after Paige's daughter Charlotte. It was a poignant reminder that we were not alone in our journey. After all, we were known as the "medical marijuana refugees,".

As the evening unfolded, laughter mingled with tears, creating a powerful tapestry of emotions. It was a moment of unity and strength as we stood together, determined to overcome the obstacles ahead and provide our children with the best possible care and support.

Paige Figi's presence was both humbling and inspiring. It was a privilege to witness firsthand the impact she had made and the sense of gratitude that filled the hearts of everyone present. Her courage in sharing Charlotte's story had not only transformed her life but had become a beacon of hope for countless others. It reinforced our sense of purpose and solidified our belief in the power of community. We were part of a movement driven by love and the pursuit of healing, and we were committed to standing shoulder-to-shoulder with these remarkable families, supporting one another every step of the way. We were the pioneers of something so new, and we needed each other more than anything.

Looking back, I am grateful for that unforgettable night around the bonfire, for it birthed a community that would touch countless lives and become a beacon of hope for families searching for answers and support. The "New Home & New Hope" Facebook group which was later launched during that time, became the first point of connection for all Colorado families who were joining the cannabis journey. It reminded us all that together, we are stronger, and our collective love has the power to transform lives.

EMPOWERED BY UNITY THROUGH THICK AND THIN

On that momentous day, filled with a mix of emotions, we embarked on a new chapter by starting Charlotte's Web. Excitement surged within us as we recognized the significance of this moment—it was the reason we had journeyed so far. This was the day we had been long anticipating. However, a lingering fear of potential ineffectiveness, based on past experiences with other medications, loomed in the background. Nevertheless, we understood the importance of staying the course and holding onto hope. After all, this was why we were here !!!

On January 3, 2014, to commemorate this milestone, Julian crafted a poster that all new families would use to capture a special photo. The sign proudly proclaimed, "OLIVIA'S FIRST DOSE," symbolizing the beginning of our journey with Charlotte's Web. With our hearts filled with hope and determination, we shared this momentous occasion by posting our first photo on the "New Home / New Hope" Facebook group, where our extended community eagerly awaited updates and celebrated our progress.

The support and encouragement we received from the group were overwhelming. Messages of solidarity and shared experiences flooded the comments section, reminding us that we were not alone in this journey. The virtual embrace of the community filled us with a renewed sense of strength and purpose. Through this simple act of posting a photo, we celebrated Olivia's first dose and built deeper connections with the families who were on the same journey.

Little did we know then how these shared experiences would shape our path moving forward. The "New Home / New Hope" Facebook group became more than just a platform for updates—it became a lifeline and a constant source of support. As we navigated the challenges of our journey together, the world that we left behind seemed to fade into the distant background. Our focus now shifted to our children's well-being and the collective support we provided one another. In this intimate circle, time seemed to stand still as we poured our hearts out, celebrated milestones, and leaned on each other during the most trying moments.

During Olivia's first week on Charlotte's Web (CW), we experienced a rollercoaster of emotions, with moments of hope and challenges along the way. As "medical marijuana refugees," we relied on our tight-knit community to support and guide us throughout this uncharted territory. Aware of the absence of neurologists endorsing CBD as a viable treatment, we took it upon ourselves to navigate this path alone, diligently making informed decisions in the best interest of our children.

Drawing upon our community's collective wisdom and shared experiences, we understood that convincing neurologists to recognize this new treatment would be an uphill battle. We embarked on a pioneering journey together, immersing ourselves in the world of cannabis to gain firsthand knowledge. United by a common purpose, we came together, exchanging stories, insights, and advice to empower one another when making dosing decisions that would profoundly impact our children's lives. Although it was a great risk, we had travelled far distances, both physically and emotionally, fully aware of the uncertain odds we faced. We were desperate and this was our only hope left.

Later in our journey, we were fortunate to cross paths with Dr. Marguerite Gedde, a remarkable physician specializing in alternative treatments. She was one of the very few physicians who actually took an interest in our subset group of patients and decided to take us all with open arms and an open heart. Her expertise and dedication to helping children like ours made her a beacon of hope in our world of uncertainty. Dr. Gedde became our guiding light throughout this challenging journey.

With genuine care and compassion, she provided invaluable support and guidance to our families. She understood the complexities of CBD treatment and the unique needs of each child, tailoring dosing schedules to suit their circumstances. Her expertise and knowledge of alternative therapies made her an invaluable resource for our community.

In the weeks and months that followed, our group interactions flourished, strengthening the bonds between us. We depended on the Colorado group of moms as it provided us with a safe space where we could voice our concerns, seek guidance, and share the joys and frustrations of our journey. Amidst the challenges we faced, we also recognized the importance of taking care of ourselves. To rejuvenate our spirits and nurture our identities, we regularly planned "mom's night out" events, allowing us to step away from our roles as caregivers, doctors, nurses, and teachers. These evenings allowed us to connect on a deeper level and to see each other as individuals with unique stories, dreams, and aspirations. After all, we were more than just moms of special needs children. We helped each other find ourselves again and rediscover the inner peace and happiness that had been buried for so long. In embracing our supportive circle, we found the courage to nurture our identities and reignite the sparks of joy and fulfillment within us. I don't know what I would have done without Paige, Nicole, Heather, and Anna. They were my rock and my saving grace. Their companionship was instrumental in shaping my experience in Colorado and creating lasting memories.

UNEXPECTED BLESSINGS

It had been six weeks since we started giving Olivia Charlotte's Web, and we experienced quite an array of emotions during this time. As we followed the advice of other parents and Dr. Gedde, we gradually increased the oils while reducing some of the pharmaceutical medications that she was taking. Little did I know that tapering off certain antiepileptic drugs would be like opening up a new can of worms. Olivia began experiencing withdrawal seizures, accompanied by heightened anxiety, agitation, and headaches. I felt utterly unprepared and helpless as I witnessed her rage and spiral out of control with anger. It was quite similar to watching a drug addict experience withdrawal symptoms. There were days when she seemed so frustrated that it seemed like she wanted to tear her own skin off. It was terrible for us to witness and endure. I can't even imagine what Olivia was feeling on the inside. It was an incredibly difficult period for all of us. However, with the unwavering support and guidance from other families who had gone through similar experiences, I found reassurance that this phase would pass with time. After four long tortuous weeks, it finally did. Olivia's happy and joyful self returned, and we were overjoyed to see her smiling face again.

Amidst the chaos of settling the children into their new schools, starting Olivia's new treatment and attending Lauren's playgroups, I completely overlooked that I hadn't had my period since arriving in Colorado. I brushed it off as stress and being busy, assuming it was just a delayed cycle. I wasn't particularly worried, but my mother insisted that I drive to the nearest pharmacy and take a pregnancy test. Without hesitation, I followed her advice and even used the pharmacy's restroom to take the test.

To my absolute astonishment, it came back positive. AHHHHHH I was pregnant! Wait, what? How could this be? I hadn't seen my husband in over six weeks, and I couldn't wrap my head around the timing. When I shared the news with my mother, she was just as shocked as I was. We sat there on the bed, silent and stunned, unable to find the right words.

My dad grew overly concerned about our prolonged silence in the bedroom and came in to check on us. My mother took it upon herself to break the news, as I was still speechless. I joked about it being the "immaculate conception," but my mother, a devout Catholic, didn't find it very amusing. The world's weight seemed to rest on my shoulders during this time in my life, and the mere thought of having another baby to care for felt utterly inconceivable. I was already battling my internal struggles and convictions, and I couldn't even fathom how to approach my husband with this insane news. I remembered how difficult it was to convince him to have Lauren, and then we were faced with his unexpected heart attack following our move to Colorado. How much more could this poor man handle? I kept the secret hidden for two days, needing time to process everything. During that time, all I could do was pray. I prayed to my God to give me the courage and strength to face this new challenge head-on, as he always did. I placed my utmost trust in Him.

Despite being 2500 km apart, Mark was always just a phone call away. We would talk multiple times a day, and I would often pour out my emotions to him, seeking his unwavering support and warm and comforting words. He always knew just what to say. However, this time was different. I couldn't hold back the deep-rooted secret any longer. It wasn't fair to either of us. On the third day after receiving the shocking news, I mustered up the courage to make him a part of this miraculous journey. I hoped he would see it the same way, but deep down, I knew how difficult it had been to convince him to have a third child. Who was I kidding? So, with trembling hands and a quivering voice, I made the call, bracing myself for his reaction. As I explained I had news for him, he automatically assumed it was about Olivia and her new treatment. But without wasting any time, I blurted out, "I'm expecting." Silence hung through the airwaves for what felt like an eternity. I grew worried and anxious until he finally responded with a comment I never saw coming.

"WHO IS THE FATHER?" I burst into hysterical laughter, unsure if he was serious or trying to process the news with humour. I reassured him that, of course, he was the father and that our busy lives with the children and my parents visiting left no room for any doubt. Not that there ever would have been, given the circumstances. His tone immediately changed, and he declared it as terrific news. I was awestruck. Where was this coming from? Was it Mark speaking? "I thought you'd be upset," I admitted. He explained that his heart attack and separation from his family had given him a newfound perspective on his life. "Maybe God has a bigger plan for us," he said. "Maybe this child was sent to us for Lauren. Who are we to deny it? Everything happens for a reason." I couldn't believe my ears. Was this truly Mark or some benevolent force that had taken over his mind? Regardless, it was a reaction a million times better than I had anticipated. I gladly embraced it and felt like the weight of this harboured secret was instantly lifted off of my shoulders. I could now breathe again and go back to focusing on what I had moved to Colorado for….Olivia.

FROM STRUGGLE TO SUPERPOWER

Mark finally made his first trip out to see us on Valentine's Day, and it was a truly special and unforgettable reunion. With my growing baby bump, a visible sign of our new pregnancy, we had a fresh perspective on life. Together, we immersed ourselves in the beauty of Colorado, making the most of our days. While Mark and Julian ventured into the mountains of Breckenridge and Vail for exhilarating skiing adventures, the girls and I leisurely strolled through the charming streets of these small towns, savouring every aspect of what Colorado had to offer. The thought of making this place our home started to take shape in our minds. We even explored the possibility of finding a house on a hill overlooking the majestic mountains. We devoted countless days to exploring various homes alongside real estate agents, immersing ourselves in the possibilities of this new chapter in our lives. Yet, a lingering question persisted: Would our Canadian passport pose a hurdle in pursuing this dream? It was an additional challenge that demanded careful consideration and meticulous planning.

The warm and welcoming people, the breathtaking landscapes, and the sunny climate all contributed to our deep appreciation for Colorado. We embraced every moment and felt grateful for the experiences we were creating together, almost knowing that it was a pipe dream.

The months in Colorado had come and gone, and Mark had made many mini trips to visit us every few weeks while the extended family would try and fill the gaps in between. We were never alone for too long as it made our time there more enjoyable and manageable. I don't know how I could have survived if I was completely on my own like other families I had met. I was blessed to have a great support system, and it was their presence and support that guided me through this journey.

Olivia was finally doing well with Charlotte's Web and we were seeing some improvement in her seizures but nothing to write home about. We knew it would be a long battle of dose adjustments with CBD oil, but we were confident that she would be on this regime for a long time. It offered the least amount of side effects with the best outcome thus far. We will take it!!

As June approached faster than we anticipated, and with the school year ending for the kids and my baby bump rapidly marking its presence, we came to the realization that our true home in Caledon was where we needed to be. While Colorado had provided us with countless treasured memories, the desire to welcome our fourth child in our home country, surrounded by our loved ones, took precedence above all else. As much as we cherished the sunny days, breathtaking mountain views, and the warmth of the local people, the longing for proximity to our family was deeply ingrained in our upbringing and essential to our very existence. Therefore without a doubt in our minds, the return flights were booked, and Olivia would continue her treatment in the comforting embrace of our familiar surroundings. Thankfully, we secured a six-month supply of CW and made the necessary arrangements to transport it back home. With everything in order, we embarked on our journey back, bidding farewell to the place that had become our temporary home for the past six months.

Parting ways with Colorado and the incredible individuals we encountered during our journey was an incredibly sad and emotional ordeal. It meant bidding farewell to the tales of familial hardships we shared and the remarkable places we explored. It meant saying goodbye to that warm unfamiliar feeling of belonging and acceptance. It meant leaving behind all the beautiful, humbled individuals who had courageously put their lives on hold on a whim that this revolutionary treatment could help their loved ones. However, on the flip side, I was forever grateful for the deepened bond within our own family that was forged through both moments of joy and of difficulty. The memories of Colorado will forever hold a special place in my heart, bidding farewell to beloved landmarks like Pikes Peak, Garden of the Gods, and Cave of the Winds. All the memories that will one day be tucked away in an old photo album on a bookshelf.

Leaving today evoked a sense of empowerment within me. All the events during this experience have shaped me into a stronger, more invincible version of myself, capable of overcoming any obstacle. I did not fully understand how or why, but I discovered a newfound confidence and power within. I felt equipped and ready to face the uncertainties that lie ahead. ***Surviving this journey with three children and a baby on the way instilled in me the belief that I can conquer anything. After all, aren't we all a result of our circumstances? Don't our life experiences shape who we are?***

OUR RAY OF SUNSHINE

Returning to our country home brought about mixed emotions. While we missed waking up to the breathtaking mountain views and the wonderful friends we had left behind, we knew that our true home resided here in Caledon, Ontario within the serenity of our 10-acre property. Our lives were constantly changing, with the impending arrival of a new baby just a few months away. Anticipation and excitement filled the air, accompanied by the natural worries of welcoming a new life into our world. Our world was already so complicated and busy. As always, we embraced these emotions with open hearts, ready to face whatever challenges lay ahead. In moments like these, I found solace in turning to my faith and seeking strength from a higher power to guide me through this journey. It became a source of comfort and guidance during challenging times.

On September 6, during the Labor Day weekend, our fourth child chose to grace us with her vibrant presence. We were surprised when she entered the world, weighing a whopping 10 lbs. We affectionately referred to her as our little butterball turkey. Like her sister Lauren, her head was adorned with a full head of dark locks. From the moment she opened her eyes, she exuded an incredible energy. Although she arrived at a time when our lives were filled with immense challenges and the difficulties of Olivia's seizures and cannabis journey, I firmly believe she came into this world with a distinct purpose.

Once again, it became evident that God had a grander plan for our family, a blueprint of what our life was meant to be in the Cancian household. Although we couldn't see the entirety of it at that moment, we trusted that everything had a purpose. The initial months with our fourth child were challenging as she grappled with discomfort and unbearable pain, leaving us feeling helpless. She had colic and those long days rolled into nights, and six months later, that phase passed. Finally, her true essence began to shine through. "Cheech", as we lovingly called her, became our source of comic relief and a beacon of sunshine. Whenever things became heavy, she would effortlessly lighten the mood with her dancing or hilarious dramatic facial expressions. Her boundless energy led many to believe she possessed superhuman athletic abilities. Even at the tender age of two, Chelsea would astound everyone with her cartwheels and flips around the gymnastics bar. Coaches couldn't help but admire her exceptional strength and agility, often remarking that she had the potential to become the next Olympian. Fast forward nine years, and Chelsea has become a proud member of a competitive gymnastics team fueled by her aspirations of Olympic success. It's truly remarkable to witness how dreams can evolve and materialize into reality as we embrace life's journey.

Chelsea, our energetic and vibrant daughter, was not only the life of every party but also the perfect companion to her older sister Lauren. Despite their contrasting personalities, they shared a special bond, like two peas in a pod. We often referred to them as "Bert and Ernie" or like "Cheech and Chong". Lauren exuded calmness and composure, always calculated and well-informed, while Chelsea embodied the spirit of fun, comical and spontaneity. Her energy, excitement, and compassion were contagious. As she grew older, her deep sense of empathy became more apparent. She profoundly loved animals, young children, individuals with special needs and the elderly. Evidently, she carried the nurturing gene passed down through generations, and nothing could hinder her from achieving great things. I was moved when she expressed her willingness to take on the role of a nanny during our search for one. She was determined to work around her school and gymnastics schedule to assist in any way she could. At that moment, it became clear to me that Chelsea was destined to be here, standing shoulder-to-shoulder with Lauren and Julian. It felt as though a master plan was unfolding before our very eyes. They were the perfect team, a united front that would guide and support us in making decisions for Olivia when we were no longer able to. The thought of their unwavering love and dedication brought immense gratitude towards God for these unexpected blessings. He had believed in me throughout our journey, and I was determined to honor His trust until the very end.

Chelsea at age 2.5

THE BUMPY ROAD TO KETOSIS

Over the years, we watched with pride as our other children grew and achieved remarkable milestones while Olivia continued to face the daily struggle of seizures and significant developmental delays. Despite her everyday use of cannabis and a few pharmaceutical medications, we struggled to find the perfect solution to eradicate her seizures. It felt like an unending marathon, but we were determined to not give up and continue to try new things. We found ourselves revisiting the two remaining options that had been presented to us in the past but hadn't been fully explored yet. It was a crucial moment, and we were ready to delve deeper into these possibilities in search of a breakthrough.

One of the options presented to us was Vagus Nerve Stimulation, a surgical procedure that involved implanting a pacemaker-like device into Olivia's vagus nerve. This device would emit gentle electrical impulses to her brain to reduce her seizures. The other option was the Ketogenic diet, a dietary plan that originated in the 1920s. It required a high-fat, low-carb eating approach. While the Ketogenic diet had shown promise in significantly reducing seizures, it came with its own set of challenges and sacrifices.

After carefully considering both options, we decided to pursue the Ketogenic diet as it was the less invasive choice. We knew how much Olivia enjoyed the food and how diligently we had worked to maintain a clean diet for her. However, if this change meant a potential reduction in her seizures, it was absolutely worth it. Desperation fueled our desire to explore all available options and give Olivia the best chance at a better quality of life. We knew what we needed to do. We just had to put our game face on and take on our next new challenge with confidence.

So in June of 2021 at the age of 15, we embarked on the ketogenic diet journey, filled with hope that it could be the missing puzzle piece in managing Olivia's seizures. From a young age, Olivia had always maintained a remarkably healthy diet, encompassing various fruits, vegetables, proteins, and whole-grain pasta. We even had her on a dairy-free and gluten-free diet for the first six years of her life which we found had a tremendous impact on her focus and concentration. Her teachers and caregivers often marvelled at her exceptional eating habits, placing bets on how much she would consume or how quickly she would finish her meals. They often found inspiration in her lunches and drew ideas for their own family dinners. Witnessing her joyful and enthusiastic approach to food was truly heartening. Watching her relish bowls of avocado and mango or savour pasta mixed with broccoli while willingly abstaining from sweets and indulgences brought us immeasurable joy. For Olivia, her clean diet became a testament to her will to thrive and prosper. It helped her navigate other challenges and strengthened her resilience against illness, boasting an unwavering immune system. Food became a source of happiness and contentment for her, and it was the only thing we had control over.

With the ketogenic diet journey underway, we were grateful to have a full-time nanny in place to assist us in preparing Olivia's meals. The journey began with a series of baseline blood tests, and then we were provided with a modified Atkins diet plan, as it seemed more manageable for us than the classic keto diet. The thought of her being confined to a hospital bed for 3-4 days and starving to achieve Ketosis didn't align with our family's needs, so the Atkins Diet was the winning choice. We started by procuring all the required supplements for Olivia's nutritional needs, which came at a significant cost. Next, we delved into the realm of specialized keto products, including MCT oil, keto snacks, and full-fat cheese and cream, among others. It was undoubtedly a departure from what we were accustomed to, but we were determined to see how this diet could potentially impact Olivia's seizures. Compared to years ago when keto products were scarce, it is now a much simpler journey to find all the necessary products at our fingertips.

We immediately embraced the keto diet, diving headfirst into a new routine that involved meticulous measurement of every morsel of food, adding full-fat cream to each meal, and a dedicated practice of monitoring Olivia's urine ketones while diligently maintaining a journal. Our days revolved around careful planning and organization, leaving no room for errors or deviations. The slightest crumb or measurement mishap could trigger additional seizures and throw her ketone levels off balance, resulting in days of regaining stability. The diet felt delicate and fragile, much like feeding a newborn or a premature baby through a tiny tube. Every ounce mattered, and the slightest excess could have detrimental effects. It was disheartening to witness Olivia's enthusiasm for eating diminish. What used to be a joyful occasion now became a painful struggle. She was hungry and irritable, longing for the foods she once enjoyed so freely. Gone were the days of endless bowls of pasta or indulging in a bowl of fresh fruit. Instead, we watched her painstakingly consume a few meagre bites, her pleading brown eyes silently begging for more. It was a challenging journey that required immense strength to persevere through. We held onto the hope that things would improve and that we would witness a reduction in seizures and an increase in alertness—ultimately achieving our desired outcome.

As the days passed, the challenges grew, and the divide between Olivia and the rest of the family became more apparent. It pained us to sit down for a family meal, indulging in delicious food, while Olivia had the meticulously measured portions that often left her unsatisfied. It was unfair for her, and the separation became increasingly evident. It was heartbreaking to see her excluded from family gatherings and social events where food was involved, especially given our Italian heritage. She was slowly becoming isolated, confined to a world that revolved around her nanny and myself. It was a difficult reality to accept, but we knew that in the grand scheme of things, her long-term well-being was our ultimate goal, and we were willing to take on this giant risk and make the necessary sacrifices for her.

Every meal became a challenge, with few moments of delight and many moments of discomfort. Her regular breakfast of bacon, eggs, cream, and cheese was undeniably delicious, but the richness often caused her to experience belly pain. I could see the longing in her eyes for the fresh fruits and veggies that used to be a staple in her diet. Personally, I struggled to fully grasp the concept of how consuming such high-fat foods could be beneficial for her in the long run. We knew the potential long-term risks, such as impacts on cholesterol levels and heart health. It made me question whether the benefits outweighed the potential drawbacks, however, we stayed on the chartered course and prayed for a miracle.

After three months on the ketogenic diet, we saw no improvement in Olivia's seizures. It was disheartening to witness her losing her zest for life, and meals became a painful experience as she would often gag at every bite. We questioned whether all the sacrifices and expenses were truly worth it. Every day, I wished that Olivia didn't have to go through this. We held onto hope, eagerly waiting for her seizures to subside, but there was no noticeable change. By the sixth month period, both the ketogenic team and I reached a consensus that the diet was deemed ineffective and not worth the immense effort and cost. Olivia's seizures remained unchanged, and her overall well-being was negatively impacted. I longed for the return of the old Olivia, the joyful and happy girl she used to be, especially during meal times. It was a reminder that her happiness and quality of life mattered the most.

In late fall 2021, we made the difficult decision to end Olivia's journey with the ketogenic diet. We gradually weaned her off the supplements and modified her eating plan, hoping to see her return to the vibrant and joyful girl she once was. While the seizures persisted, our main focus was to have Olivia back in our lives, embracing her true self. We came to the realization that the ketogenic diet didn't provide the outcomes we had hoped for, and we marked it off our list of options. However, we remained open to exploring VNS (Vagus Nerve Stimulation) as a potential treatment down the road. *At present, our main priority is to treasure every moment with Olivia and witness her living her life to the absolute fullest, embracing her individual path. We cherish each and every moment with her, knowing that our unconditional love and support were the greatest gifts we could offer.*

ANGELS IN SCRUBS

We were incredibly fortunate to have Becky as our hygienist at the clinic, BRITE BITE in Vaughan, Ontario from when Olivia was 10. In my eyes, she was like another angel sent from the heavens above to make Olivia's earthly journey as meaningful as possible. Her deep compassion for children with special needs made her truly remarkable. Perhaps it was influenced by having an autistic brother of her own or her naturally gentle and patient demeanor. Regardless, we felt blessed to have her. Every three months, we eagerly looked forward to our appointments with Becky. Alongside her, we were equally fortunate to have Sandi, the office manager, who would purposely leave her front desk job to be present at every appointment, singing songs and ensuring that Olivia felt loved and supported.

Here's how the appointment would go: I would arrive at the clinic and wait in my truck with Olivia. Once the room was ready for us, we would receive special treatment—an exclusive back-door service that led us to a soundproof room equipped with screens cued and ready to play Olivia's favourite shows or movies. The Wiggles were always the favourite. When we entered the dental room, I would take the first seat on the dental chair and lay right down on my back. Olivia would then proceed to lie directly on top of me. Our legs would intertwine, and my arms would wrap around hers, creating a secure and comforting embrace. Sandi would gently hold her head in place while Becky, our dedicated dental hygienist, would patiently attend to Olivia's teeth. Olivia wasn't always the most cooperative child when it came to opening her mouth for Becky's work. In the early years, she would sometimes scream at the top of her lungs, but Becky so graciously remained committed and determined. Like she was meant to do this. A true godsend. We all understood that this was the procedure that Olivia resisted the most, given her easy going nature, so we did everything in our power to make it a comfortable and an enjoyable experience for her. We all sang along in unison to a personalized playlist. Harmonizing our voices, we created a soothing atmosphere to help Olivia relax, and in turn, we were all united in a common purpose. When she resisted, it often meant singing our songs louder or taking many necessary breaks for her to relax and regain composure. It was a true team effort, with everyone working together to prioritize Olivia's well-being and ensure she received the dental care she needed.

The impact of this approach has been life-changing. Today, Olivia willingly attends dental appointments and cooperates with Becky by independently opening her mouth for examination with little assistance by Sandi. Although she still lays on top of me with her 85-pound body and long spaghetti legs, we have come a long way. Becky and Sandi have been amazing in their care for Olivia. The trust and bond we've developed with them have truly transformed Olivia's life. I can't express enough how grateful I am for their exceptional dedication. It's people like them who make a profound impact on the lives of these special children like Olivia, and I am forever indebted to their compassion and commitment.

HEAVENLY HELPERS

Raising children, especially those with special needs, truly requires a village. Reflecting on my 17 years, I can confidently assert that accepting help and recognizing the need for a team of specialized individuals is crucial for maintaining happiness and sanity at home. Fortunately, I had the means to take on assistance in raising my children while navigating Olivia's challenges, but the significant challenge always lay in finding the right person for the job. We were incredibly fortunate to come across exceptional individuals over the course of Olivia's life. Mona, our first nanny, joined us when Olivia was just one and a half years old and started her ACTH steroid treatment. What was initially meant to be a three-month arrangement extended to an incredible seven years, from full-time to part-time. Witnessing these extraordinary individuals put their families on hold to assist us selflessly was awe-inspiring. It made me reflect on how fortunate we were to have been born on this side of the world, where we didn't have to make such life-altering decisions. The thought of leaving my young family behind to be raised by their father or grandparents while I ventured across the globe to make a living was unimaginable. The thought of not being a part of my children's everyday lives, was just too much to bear, yet they so selflessly and courageously take on this sacrifice with open arms. Mona holds a beautiful place in my heart as her time spent with Olivia was irreplaceable. Her bond was undeniable, and although Olivia may not remember her, we will never forget her love and genuine care for all of us. She has since reunited with her family years later and began a wonderful life of her own.

Mona and Olivia at age 2

Let me introduce you to Shelly, an extraordinary individual who seamlessly became a part of our family shortly after Chelsea was born. Over the past ten years, I can't adequately convey just how remarkable she is and how much she means to each and every one of us. Shelly has been a lifeline, offering invaluable support and evolving into a cherished member of our extended family. Initially joining us as a full-time nanny, she later transitioned into a part-time helper. The bond between all my children and Shelly is exceptional—they view her as a second mother, and their love and connection are heartwarming. Having her around brings a sense of trust and warmth into our home. She has been our rock during the toughest of times, helping us navigate challenges as a united family. She goes above and beyond her role as a caregiver, embracing us as her own family. However as time went on, Olivia's needs grew more intricate. The two days a week that Shelly devoted to our family wasn't enough to handle the growing needs of Olivia. Her skills began to regress due to a prolonged time of uncontrolled seizures. Walking became progressively challenging, and she developed a heightened sensitivity to loud noises and chaos. Our home's natural acoustics, inherently noisy, posed a considerable challenge in creating an environment suitable for Olivia. Segregating Olivia from the rest of the family became an ongoing battle as she increasingly needed more constant one-on-one attention for almost every aspect of her daily activities. As Lauren and Chelsea's interests and activities outside school began to flourish, I found myself in a challenging situation. More often than not, I would bring Olivia along to their events, only to witness her endure a seizure amidst the crowd, drawing unwanted attention and concern. This situation was both exasperating and heart-wrenching. In an attempt to navigate this, I started to stay back in the car with Olivia, which, in turn, left the girls disheartened by our absence at their events. It felt like I was caught in a relentless bind, facing a dilemma with no right answer. Every choice seemed to lead to disappointment for someone.

The balancing act of catering to Olivia's needs while trying to support my other children's busy schedules was draining. The quest for a solution that could bring some form of happiness to everyone seemed like a distant dream. The burden of this responsibility was immense, making me feel as though I was entrenched in a situation with no viable way out. I was desperate for a way to ease this strain but was uncertain about where to begin.

Shelly and Olivia at age 17.

Just when I thought I was at my wit's end, and it couldn't get any harder, God had a unique way to show me that things needed to change. In June 2020, as I hurriedly prepared the girls for our weekend trip to the summer cottage, an unexpected incident that would influence my decision for a lifetime unfolded. While showering Olivia and rushing to get her dressed, she slipped and fell, landing face-first on the tiles. It was a moment of sheer panic and tears as she cried like never before. Despite our attempts to assess her pain, we attributed her discomfort to the fear of the fall itself and she soon calmed down. Determined to stick to our scheduled departure, the family loaded up the SUV and off we went. Olivia remained quite unsettled in the truck and began to whimper which quickly turned into inconsolable crying throughout the entire journey. This was entirely out of character, raising our concern. Upon reaching our destination, It became evident to all of us that something serious had occurred to Olivia. Without any delay, we rushed her to the local emergency room in Midland, Ontario. Despite enduring a lengthy wait in triage, the medical team eventually conducted a comprehensive examination, confirming our worst fear—Olivia had a broken collarbone. This news hit me hard, especially since school had just ended, and the summer was supposed to be a time of joy and relaxation.

"Bring it on, baby," I whispered to myself. Feeling utterly disappointed and angry, I tried to muster up the courage and strength to face this new challenge with positivity. Armed with painkillers and a sling, we returned back to the cottage, but Olivia was uncooperative and adamantly refused to wear the splint, adding to our frustration. It left me pondering how to provide her care while being there for my other three children, especially as summer had just begun. At that point, Shelly could only come twice a week, and it simply wasn't enough support for us.

The weight of the situation began to bear heavily on me. I felt torn between being the best caregiver for Olivia and fulfilling my responsibilities to my other children. Juggling everything and ensuring each of them received the attention and care they deserved seemed impossible.

Regrettably, we were finding ourselves repeatedly witnessing Olivia enduring severe grand mal seizures, often occurring during our family dinners. These seizures would disrupt our everyday conversations, accompanied by the clattering of cutlery against plates and the occasional clash of drinking glasses on the glass table. Despite our best efforts, these unavoidable and uncontrollable noises seemed to distress Olivia, triggering these terrifying episodes. Witnessing her suffering was heart-wrenching, and it profoundly affected my other children. They would lose their appetite and feel overwhelmed with sadness at having seen such distressing moments. Exposing them to this reality felt unjust, but we couldn't deny that it had become a part of our lives—it was our reality.

The days became increasingly challenging as I endeavoured to juggle the responsibilities of being a mother to neurotypical children while also being a mother to a special needs daughter who required constant one-on-one attention. Wearing both hats, it felt like an ongoing battle, and I grappled with guilt. The notion of hiring a full-time nanny solely dedicated to Olivia's care weighed heavily on my conscience. I questioned whether seeking additional help meant I was somehow giving up on her or failing as a mother. Deep within, I acknowledged the urgent necessity for a transformation to ensure the welfare of our entire family. I knew prompt action was essential to avoid potential negative repercussions.

SURVIVING NOT THRIVING

I had an upcoming appointment with my favourite physician, Dr. David Chitayat, who had become our designated metabolic specialist and showed great interest in Olivia's case. Over the years, he had dedicated countless hours to conducting whole genome scans and various tests to find a distinct diagnosis for Olivia. Unfortunately, the results pointed to a rare sporadic genetic mutation that gave us little direction or prognosis.

Despite our challenges, our visits with Dr. Chitayat were always memorable. He had a cheerful demeanor and genuinely cared about our well-being. I looked forward to our appointments because he took a considerable amount of time to listen to the latest happenings in our lives. However, during one particular visit, Dr. Chitayat surprised me by starting the appointment with questions about Mark's well-being. Mark rarely accompanied me to these appointments due to his work commitments, and I had never expected him to be there. Yet in honesty, it was becoming increasingly challenging for me to handle these appointments alone.

I was taken aback by Dr. Chitayat's focus on our relationship and how we were doing rather than solely discussing Olivia's genetic condition. It was a pleasant surprise, and it made me feel seen and supported in a way I hadn't expected. I quickly assured him that Mark was okay without divulging too much information and apologized for his absence, attributing it to his work obligations. However, Dr. Chitayat continued to delve into personal matters, asking about our recent travels together and the state of our marriage. I couldn't comprehend why he was interested in these personal details. What did they have to do with Olivia's genetic condition? I pondered this silently. I responded by saying that things were okay between us and how we struggled to find time together without the constant demands of our four children. That's when Dr. Chitayat abruptly interrupted me, exclaiming, "SO WHAT!"

He went on to share an alarming statistic of 90% of marriages that fail due to the fact that they had special needs children. What struck me most was what he said next. His observation was that these mothers, while dedicating a significant amount of time, money, and energy to care for their special needs child, unintentionally neglected their spouses and other neurotypical children. He cautioned me about the potential consequences of this neglect, emphasizing that it could result in significant behavioural issues for the overlooked children in the future, as they might feel abandoned and unnoticed. The looming problem was set to be much more challenging to endure.

He emphasized that while a special needs child might progress more slowly, as long as their needs were met, they could still find happiness. Dr. Chitayat drew an intriguing analogy, comparing our daughter Olivia to a golden retriever. Curious, I attentively listened to his narrative, seeking to grasp the essence of the comparison.

He explained that the dog may initially feel melancholy when a golden retriever's owner departs. However, if a new caretaker steps in, expressing love and providing sustenance, treats, and playtime, the dog eventually returns to a happy state without harbouring any resentment toward the original owner.

This analogy prompted me to pause and reflect. It made me realize that while prioritizing Olivia's needs is crucial, we must also ensure we don't neglect our other children and marriage. Olivia's happiness remains unwavering as long as her needs are fully addressed. It doesn't matter if it's me, our nanny, a teacher, or a babysitter – as long as she is surrounded by kind and compassionate individuals who prioritize her well-being, she exudes joy. Olivia's happiness mirrors the love and care she receives from those around her.

Therefore, he emphasized that finding a balance is paramount, ensuring everyone in the family feels loved and cared for. It won't be effortless, but by being mindful of each other's needs and nurturing your relationships, you can cultivate a harmonious and joyful home for everyone involved.

Dr. Chitayat encouraged me to retake charge and invest the necessary time in building a solid relationship with my husband again, as he believed it was crucial for the foundation of our family. He also urged me to try to go on mini trips or engage in experiences with my other children, creating bonds and memories that they would cherish for a lifetime. He explained that my other children needed me more than Olivia did. He stressed the importance of letting go and hiring full-time help to relieve the burden I had carried for so long. He could see that I was merely surviving, not thriving, and it was a realization I hadn't fully grasped until he pointed it out with such clarity. I had been consumed with meeting Olivia's needs for so long, inadvertently neglecting the needs of everyone else in the process.

Leaving the appointment with Dr. Chitayat, his words resonated deeply in my mind. Was it time to relinquish the burden of caring for Olivia and entrust her to someone skilled and more patient? The ride home was filled with introspection as I contemplated his perspective. Though daunting, the idea of seeking full-time help for Olivia's care and focusing on the well-being of our entire family took root within me. Dr. Chitayat's advice opened my eyes to the importance of nurturing the bonds within our family and tending to my relationship with Mark. Was it time to reevaluate and find the right support system for Olivia, a step towards creating a healthier balance and ensuring she received the care she truly deserved?

Maybe he was right!

DECIDING HER DESTINY

After many heartfelt discussions with the family, Mark and I reached a pivotal decision following Olivia's broken collarbone incident. It became evident that this was Allan's way of communicating to us, a clear sign that a change was necessary. We couldn't continue subjecting Olivia to overwhelming stimuli day after day. It was a bitter pill to swallow, as a part of me yearned for her constant presence, longing for a sense of completeness within our family unit. Yet, deep down, I knew it wasn't in her best interest. As a teenager, she needed her space as Julian did. We had to come to terms with the fact that she had outgrown being treated as a little girl and prioritize what would truly benefit her, even if it meant adjusting our expectations. It took me 14 years to fully embrace this wave of change, but the conversation with Dr. Chitayat brought newfound clarity. I had to release myself from the burden of guilt and embrace the reality that Olivia's purpose on this earth differed from ours. She existed in a different dimension, with her unique journey to navigate alongside us. While she may not be actively involved in our day-to-day activities, finding solace in her pursuit of happiness and safety should satisfy us. ***I had to let go of the quest for perfection and instead embrace the concept of progress.*** It was no easy task, but it was vital for us to coexist with Olivia in this world. ***Her world may appear different, but who are we to claim ours is better? Her life is free from judgment and jealousy, a pure and joyful existence untethered by stress. Like a butterfly spreading its wings and soaring high above, she gracefully navigates her own path, unaffected by the troubles and predators of the world.***

Thus, we commenced the quest for a full-time nanny capable of tending to all of Olivia's needs, enabling me to redirect my attention to the activities and commitments of my other children that had been deferred for so long. Along came Edna, whose proficiency in assisting a young adult using a wheelchair made her seem like the ideal match for Olivia. While it took some time for her to acclimate to Olivia's daily routine and distinctive characteristics, a profound sense of relief washed over me once she mastered it. I cannot adequately convey the deep mental and physical liberation I experienced. It was genuinely astonishing to realize the magnitude of the stress I had been shouldering without even being aware of it. My sleep improved, the tension in my body decreased, headaches became less frequent, and overall, I found myself authentically happier. It felt like a decade had been added to my life with a mere finger snap. This remarkable transformation served as a potent reminder of the significance of finding the right support and embracing self-care.

With having nannies comes the harsh reality of contracts and limited durations. Two years can pass by in the blink of an eye. After investing in their sponsorships and becoming accustomed to their presence in our home, their time eventually concluded, and we found ourselves back at square one. Unfortunately, Edna's tenure with us had ended as she obtained an open work permit, granting her the freedom to pursue any job in the country and apply for permanent residency. Most international nannies' primary goal is to bring over their family, from whom they had been separated. Witnessing such selflessness and personal sacrifice is truly admirable. Edna deserved all the happiness in the world, however, her departure left me with the challenge of finding another caregiver to meet Olivia's increasing needs. At nearly 17 years old, Olivia had grown significantly, standing almost as tall as me at 5'5". Her physical abilities had regressed over the past year or two, making it challenging to navigate stairs. Her speech had also declined, with only a few repetitive words remaining in her vocabulary. She continued to experience 1-2 seizures daily, requiring full-time assistance in nearly every activity. Finding a caregiver willing to meet those specific needs and live in the rural area of Caledon, where transportation was limited, seemed impossible. Additionally, our nannies typically work on weekends and take their days off during weekdays, adding another obstacle to the equation.

After numerous attempts and disappointments, we found ourselves feeling helpless and overwhelmed. The task of finding a suitable nanny for our precious daughter had become far more challenging than we had anticipated. Doubts started to creep in. Many scenarios began to surface in our brains. Would we ever find someone we could trust to care for our fragile Olivia? Should we consider relocating to an area with better transportation options? Should we hire multiple nannies to cover weekdays and weekends? Was it time to explore the possibility of a full-time residence for her? These weighty questions left us at a crossroads, uncertain about the best path for Olivia's future.

Amidst the confusion, we turned to our instincts and followed our hearts. Deep down, we knew we couldn't bear the thought of being separated from Olivia, not yet. We cherished every moment with her, from bedtime kisses and lullabies to being attuned to her emotions and needs. The thought of letting go of those precious connections was unimaginable for us. Instead, we resolved to persist in our search for the right nanny and explore new housing options that would better cater to Olivia's needs. Whether it meant finding a home with an elevator or a separate walk-out entrance, we were determined to make it work. Having her with us was as essential for us as we believed it was for her. I needed to be attuned to her happiness and recognize when she faced challenging days. It was all indispensable, and I wasn't prepared to relinquish any of it. Olivia was our daughter, our lifelong responsibility, and as long as we had control over it, we wanted her to be with us.

The journey was far from easy, and the road ahead remained uncertain. However, we clung to the belief that we could find a solution allowing Olivia to thrive while keeping our family unit intact. We knew it would demand patience, persistence, and a readiness to adapt, but our love for Olivia and our commitment to her well-being would guide us through the challenges ahead, as it always did.

Finding a new nanny became a difficult task to endure. After trialling five separate candidates in a six-week period, we luckily encountered a special lady by the name of Hyde who travelled across Canada to step into some big shoes. Although she wasn't extensively trained in working with individuals with special needs, her determination to care for Olivia and prioritize her well-being was quickly evident and embraced.

Later, we embarked on the quest for a new home, an endeavour that often felt like an uphill battle. However, we clung to the belief that, somehow, the universe was aligning in our favour. Miraculously, the following day, we chanced upon a bungalow that felt tailor-made for our family. This place exuded undeniable charm, enveloped by lush greenery and featuring a tranquil pond reminiscent of the serene property we had left behind. What truly set it apart was the separate living area meticulously designed for

Olivia and the nanny. It was a space devoid of stairs and uneven surfaces—a sanctuary where she could thrive and reconnect with nature, finding the solace and inner peace she had always sought.

As we explored the rooms, a renewed sense of hope washed over us. It felt like the stars had aligned, and we couldn't shake the notion that Mark's late brother, Allan, played a role in guiding us to this extraordinary outcome. His spirit seemed to linger in the subtle synchronicities that led us to this perfect home. Deeply grateful for the unseen forces orchestrating this remarkable journey, it reaffirmed our belief that there is a greater plan at work beyond our comprehension.

Our journey took an exciting turn when we found a place we could finally call home, providing Olivia with the love, support, and understanding she truly deserved. However, this decision came with its own set of challenges. Our other children were understandably hesitant about leaving their familiar neighbourhood and friends behind. We had built strong connections with our community, and the thought of starting over was daunting. Emotionally, I felt torn. I had almost grown accustomed to a lack of normalcy, and the concept of routine and stability seemed unattainable. I knew prioritizing Olivia's needs was essential, but at what cost? Were other families facing similar decisions as frequently as we were? Life with a special needs child was undeniably difficult, and it often felt like we were constantly being tested to measure our resilience and adaptability to change.

As parents, we had to make tough choices and prioritize the well-being of our entire family, even if it meant stepping out of our comfort zones. We understood that a physical location didn't define true home, but by the values and connections we shared as a family. It was our experiences in the home that made us who we were. Resilience became our guiding light, reminding us that material possessions may come and go, but the unbreakable bonds we had formed as a family would always endure. With hope in our hearts and a renewed sense of purpose, we embraced our eighth home together, hoping to cherish every precious moment spent with Olivia in her newfound sanctuary. It was a testament to our unwavering commitment as parents to a special needs child, driven by love and a deep desire to provide a nurturing environment for our beloved daughter.

Olivia with Edna, her first full-time nanny at age 14.

GRIEF KNOWS NO BOUNDARIES

One of the profound lessons I've learned in parenting a special needs child is that grief knows no boundaries or has no expiration. It resurfaces at different stages in life, catching us off guard just when we thought we had moved past it. It's an ongoing process. When we pour our hearts and souls into our child, making sacrifices without seeing the desired outcomes, that's grief. When our lives have revolved around ticking off boxes of achievement, and our child doesn't fit into those expected milestones, that's grief. When we turn to the doctor in search of hope for new treatments or a prognosis, only to find ourselves confronted with unanswered questions and uncertainty, it's like facing another wave of grief crashing over us. Grief, in its various forms, will inevitably touch each of us. It becomes a personal journey, a life lesson, to learn how to coexist with this dreadful emotion and to find the inner strength to rise above it. Even when the hurdles in our path seem insurmountable, we must strive to propel forward.

As parents, we often measure our own self-worth and success based on our ability to overcome challenges and fulfill societal expectations. But parenting a special needs child goes against all conventional notions. It has its own set of rules. It forces us to redefine success, detach ourselves from this notion of what is normal embrace small victories, and find strength in moments of connection and love. Grief becomes intertwined with resilience, and we learn to navigate the complexities of our emotions, holding onto hope while cherishing every precious moment with our child.

Despite Olivia's current circumstances, which differ from the path I had imagined for her, she remains resilient. Although she faces continuous challenges with speech, motor skills, and seizures and still requires support for most of her daily tasks, her spirit shines through. Even in the midst of darkness, her eyes sparkle with life, her heart overflows with love, and a radiant smile breaks through. It's these glimpses of light that inspire us to persevere, to continue dreaming, praying, and hoping for a brighter future. Olivia teaches us the invaluable lesson of resilience, reminding us to never surrender, even when the journey seems daunting.

REINVENTING YOURSELF

How can we maintain a sense of joy and happiness when our world often feels like it's falling apart? As we navigate the challenges and trials that come our way each day, finding a way to live and coexist becomes an ongoing pursuit. Over the years, I have discovered several strategies that have helped me propel forward and find happiness amidst the chaos. It has been a journey of 17 years and counting, but these practices have allowed me to cope with and overcome numerous obstacles with a sense of calm and confidence.

FORGETTING THE OLD YOU

There are moments when we find ourselves longing for our old selves, those days of innocence and ignorance when we didn't know the depths of pain and suffering. Our lives were different back then, without the experiences we carry now. I recall a particular day while driving with Olivia and Julian in the car. I witnessed Olivia experiencing a grand mal seizure in the back seat while Julian cried in distress. The feeling of helplessness washed over me as I desperately wished to stop my truck to ease their suffering and offer comfort. At a stoplight, I glanced to my left and saw a young attractive girl, probably just a few years younger than me, driving a vibrant convertible MINI COOPER. She had the music blaring and was applying lipstick in the rearview mirror, joyfully singing along to the lyrics with a radiant smile. She seemed so carefree, unaware of the challenges that awaited her in the future. It led me to contemplate my past and desire the simplicity I once enjoyed when my life centered around my own passions, interests, and personal pursuits. The nostalgia for those days was strong, but I soon realized that dwelling on the past would hinder my ability to embrace and accept my present reality. I needed to let go of what once was and focus on the opportunities and growth that awaited me in my new life. I will never seem to forget that day, but it provided me with the perspective I needed to appreciate my current reality.

BECOME A MASTERY AT SOMETHING

When our world feels chaotic and out of control, seeking solace or distraction through overcompensation in other areas of our lives is common. Some may turn to temporary escapes like alcohol or drugs, while others find comfort in indulging in food and other pleasures. However, this is an opportunity to redirect that energy towards positive endeavours that benefit ourselves and potentially impact others. I realized that immersing myself in new skills and hobbies brought my life a renewed sense of purpose and fulfillment. In the calm of our country home, I embarked on a new venture by turning the coach house into a small fashion boutique. This allowed me to unleash the creative energy that I had inherited from my mom and share my passion for fashion with others.

The connections I made and the friendships that blossomed from this endeavor brought me a deep sense of joy and gratification. I became known as the fashionista of our little town of Caledon, and knowing that I could help others and do what I love, began to fill my once emptied cup.

I had to relinquish the idea of trying to change things. In the face of uncontrollable circumstances, I had to shift my focus toward the things I had control over. By immersing myself in my passions and pursuits, I found an escape from the burdens and challenges that often overwhelmed me. This journey of personal growth brought me a sense of solace and happiness and allowed me to embrace a more relaxed and fulfilled outlook on life. Along the way, I forged meaningful connections and discovered the power of pursuing what truly mattered to me, ultimately leading to a greater sense of purpose and fulfillment.

ACCEPTING HELP

Accepting full-time help for my daughter was one of the most challenging yet essential decisions I had to make. It took me 14 years to realize that this journey was not meant for me to navigate alone. I didn't want to become a martyr or expect any recognition in the end. These extraordinary children were entrusted to us with a purpose, and there was no manual to guide us through it. Recognizing the essential role of community support, I accepted that my child's true potential could only be unlocked through the combined efforts of those around us. By embracing this truth, we can find greater happiness and fulfillment, knowing that we are earthly guardians responsible for guiding them through a world filled with challenges until they ultimately reach a realm free from pain and suffering.

CALMING THE CHAOS THROUGH SELF-CARE

Chaos is an inevitable part of our lives, but our response to it ultimately shapes our outcomes. While meditation has been a continuous challenge for me, I aspire to conquer it in the future. However, yoga has always been my saving grace. Through years of practice, I have learned to quiet my mind and find solace. Even on the most challenging days, a single yoga class can rejuvenate my spirit, preparing me to face any obstacles that come my way. Alongside yoga, I have discovered the value of connecting with like-minded individuals by joining a small women's fitness group and embracing the running world. These activities have provided me with inner calm amidst the chaos. Despite not being naturally inclined towards physical activity, I have become a testament to the possibility of personal transformation. I realized the importance of dedicating time to myself, finding a healthy escape, and experiencing the camaraderie of others who share similar triumphs and struggles. Engaging in these activities allows me to let go of the things beyond my control and focus on prioritizing my physical and mental well-being.

I also realized the profound impact of an organized home on my state of mind. Being an "A Type" personality, I found tremendous joy in keeping my space tidy and embracing the art of decorating. Creating an organized and harmonious environment became a sanctuary for my family and me, offering a respite of peace and tranquillity amidst the chaos of our daily lives.

THE ART OF COMPARTMENTALIZATIONS

Mastering the art of compartmentalization has been a gradual and crucial journey for maintaining my mental well-being, particularly with the complexities of managing a large family that includes a special needs child. Leveraging my Type-A personality, I established a structured schedule and routine to stay organized and focused. However, I soon realized that I couldn't navigate this journey alone. Opening myself up and trusting others, including teachers, friends, family, and nannies, enabled me to create mental space for different responsibilities.

Being physically present in multiple places simultaneously is an impossibility for a parent. Therefore, prioritizing tasks and responsibilities became a vital skill. This lesson instilled patience in my children from an early age. Our family functions as a cohesive unit with diverse needs and aspirations. Emphasizing the importance of teamwork became our guiding principle for fostering harmony at home. Everyone is treated equally, and I maintain a zero-tolerance policy regarding impatience or entitlement. My ultimate goal is to raise responsible and compassionate adults who can confidently navigate the world around them, devoid of entitlement and privilege.

When I dedicate one-on-one time to each child, my focus is solely on them. I want them to feel cherished and unique during our special date nights. Simultaneously, I ensure the other children are well taken care of. Striking this balance fosters unity and consideration within our family. I transition between these roles, mentally shifting gears to give my full attention. It is almost like mentally flipping switches. For example, when I watch Olivia board the bus in the mornings, a sense of relief washes over me as I mentally transfer responsibility to the bus driver. Almost as though I am passing the torch of accountability to the driver. I have to place complete trust in them that Olivia gets delivered safely to the teacher in order for me to release any worries on my mind. It is like a transfer of power. A wholehearted letting go. I can then effectively shift my focus to the next child, preparing them for the day. This practice, though challenging at times, allows me to keep going. Focusing on one task at a time, I declutter my mind, staying organized and focused throughout the day.

Compartmentalization is the key to bringing order and mental freedom into my life. It's as if I have a personal filing cabinet in my mind where I can neatly store away tasks, thoughts, and emotions for later use. This practice allows me to effectively manage stress, anxiety, and distractions by organizing them into distinct compartments.

By compartmentalizing, I enhance my productivity and focus on one aspect of my life at a time. This approach brings clarity, control, and the ability to be present and savour precious moments with my children fully. It enables me to dedicate quality time to each task or interaction without being overwhelmed by other responsibilities.

Moreover, it empowers me to maintain balance in my life. It ensures that I allocate time for myself and engage in activities that bring me happiness and fulfillment.

ACCEPTING GROWTH SHOULD BE PROGRESS, NOT PERFECTION

Realizing the need to let go of perfection was a significant turning point in my journey. For the first seven years of Olivia's life, I desperately tried to mould her into what I thought was the ideal version of herself, constantly comparing her to others and feeling frustrated with our challenges. I was chasing *normal,* constantly finding myself disappointed. However, as time passed, I learned the valuable lesson that *progress,* not *perfection,* was the key.

Imagine facing a massive rock obstructing your path, wedged tightly between a towering cliff and a steep mountain. That rock symbolizes our challenges in shaping Olivia's future according to our preconceived notions. I struggled to move that immovable rock for years, desperately trying to conform to societal norms. But eventually, I realized that my efforts were in vain. Instead of persistently pushing against the rock, I needed to change my perspective and explore alternative routes to reach my goals. It meant embracing Olivia's uniqueness and finding ways to navigate the obstacles, whether it was finding a ladder to climb over the rock or swinging through the trees to reach the other side. It was a transformative shift in my mindset, realizing that striving for progress and embracing our individuality held greater value than chasing an elusive idea of perfection. I let go of the pursuit of normalcy and instead chose to redefine my rules to live by. ***This meant embracing imperfections, celebrating uniqueness, and finding fulfillment in the journey rather than the destination. By breaking free from societal expectations and charting my own path, I discovered the true meaning of success and happiness. It was about embracing my authentic self, embracing change, and embracing the beauty of a life lived on my terms.***

LETTING GO OF GUILT

Overcoming feelings of guilt can be particularly challenging, especially when family values and traditions are deeply rooted and ingrained, as is often the case in families of European descent.

As I officially enter the sandwich generation, I constantly find myself torn between fulfilling the day-to-day needs of my own family and the added weight of guilt for not being fully present and available to our aging parents. The desire to satisfy others and ensure their happiness has always been a defining trait of mine, but it can also feel like a heavy load to bear.

As time passes and our parents grow older, the guilt of not being physically present and readily available for them becomes increasingly strong. It's a complex emotional struggle, navigating the responsibilities and obligations we feel towards our own immediate family while also trying to honour and support our parents. Finding a balance that respects our own well-being and the needs of our loved ones can be a delicate balancing act.

It's important to recognize that we are only human and cannot be in multiple places at once. Accepting that we have limitations and learning to prioritize our own family's needs while also finding ways to stay connected and involved with our parents can help alleviate some of the guilt and learn to let go. Regular communication, expressing our love and concern, and making the most of the time we have together can go a long way in maintaining solid bonds and easing the burden of guilt.

LOVING YOURSELF

From an early age, my loving parents instilled in me a powerful belief: that I was special and unique. Their constant reminders of my worth and individuality laid the foundation for a strong sense of identity. I carried this confidence with me as I grew, proud of the person I had become—a devoted daughter, a loyal friend, a loving wife, and a dedicated mother. Even on my toughest days, I found solace in the knowledge that I was doing my best and always had faith in the decisions I made. I felt bulletproof, and "BRING IT ON BABY", my motto, became a declaration of my determination to face any obstacle that came my way. Having a supportive and loving husband only added fuel to the fire within me, as his unwavering belief in my abilities ignited my personal strength and sense of control. Mark always reassured me that together we can face any hurdle and that anything was possible. Together, we built a partnership rooted in trust and mutual support, empowering me to face life's challenges with determination.

Today, I proudly instill this same confidence and self-love in my children. Nurturing their sense of self-assurance will empower them to overcome obstacles and thrive in every aspect of their lives. By teaching them to believe in themselves and their abilities, I hope to equip them with the tools to succeed and persevere, no matter their challenges. It is my greatest hope that they carry this unwavering confidence with them throughout their life's journey, embracing their uniqueness and welcoming the uncertainty of the world with open arms.

GIVING BACK

There has always been this strong urge within me to give back, to repay the kindness and support I have received throughout the years. It's as if I felt a sense of responsibility, a need to balance the scales. To give back to the world that offered me such great help in the times I needed it most, with incredible individuals like Mona, Shelly, Edna, and now Hyde. I felt an overwhelming gratitude, and I wanted to channel that internal flame by making a positive impact on the lives of others. This desire to give back took on various forms for me. One of the ways I started was by volunteering to deliver meals to the elderly. It was not just about the satisfaction of providing them with nourishment; it was the conversations and connections that blossomed during those visits that truly touched me. I realized that deep within me, there was a burning desire to assist and support others. There was an inner voice urging me to do great things, and I couldn't ignore it any longer.

After years of volunteering for different events at our local Caledon Community Services, something incredible happened. I was offered a part-time position after 18 years of being a stay-at-home mother, to lead the town events for the organization. I can't express how elated I was to finally be recognized for my skills and have the opportunity to continue making a difference. Taking on this role allowed me to truly immerse myself in the community, and it opened my eyes to the struggles that many people in our town face. It reminded me that I was not alone in my journey. There were many people alongside us, fighting their own inner demons and dealing with heartache and misfortune. I discovered that I had the power to make a difference in such a small town. Embracing this new chapter of my life brought me a deep sense of purpose and fulfillment. Giving back to others became more than just a responsibility; it became ingrained in my identity. It gave me a sense of belonging and reaffirmed my belief in the transformative power of compassion and support. Most importantly, it allowed me to show my children the importance of being selfless and positively impacting by leading through example.

UNDERSTANDING THE MISUNDERSTOOD

Each special person that comes into this complicated world has a way of connecting with the universe around them, guiding them through their earthly journey. For Olivia, her connection to the world comes alive through music, motion and her infectious smile. We've discovered the incredible power of music in enhancing Olivia's everyday experiences. Whether it's brushing her teeth or going down the stairs, we are constantly incorporating melodies into these seemingly ordinary activities, giving Olivia a unique way to express herself. She comes alive, and her eyes are open wide to the world when the sound of songs meets her eardrums. We're fortunate to have a music therapist visit our home in the summer months. They bring an array of instruments, inviting Olivia to explore new sounds and rhythms, creating a delightful and engaging musical journey. It's a time of pure joy and release for Olivia as she immerses herself in the magical world of music, her happy place.

The movement also plays a significant role in her life, whether enjoying the gentle sway of a swing or hammock or the exhilarating boat rides in the summer. Many therapists refer to this as "movement therapy." This type of motion offers her a chance to unwind and find respite from the sensory overload of her surroundings. Observing her on the boat, with her head moving along the rhythm of the waves, her arms swaying in the air, and a wide grin on her face feels like a symphony playing before our eyes. She's in her own element, where she's meant to be. I still remember the adorable way she used to say, "Look at the BIIIIIIIIIGGGGG BOATS" when she was younger, and it always brought us all to fits of laughter. The wonder in her eyes and the serenity in her body language during these moments remind us that she's truly embracing the best life she can live.

Lastly, Olivia's smile is a profound glimpse into her soul. Without uttering a single word, it communicates her emotions and reveals what brings her true happiness. It transcends language and goes beyond mere words or phrases. It is a pure and genuine expression that emerges when Olivia is immersed in her world, experiencing the things that make her heart sing.

Her teachers are often amazed by the power of her smile. They recognize that it is a valuable tool in helping them understand her wants and desires. Through her radiant smile, Olivia can convey her needs and joy, forging a deeper connection with those around her. It is a testament to the unique way she interacts with the world, reminding us of the beauty and power of non-verbal communication.

Olivia living her best life as she enjoys the wind and movement of the boat at age 8

Her eyes are the gateway to her soul (age 10)

Olivia strolling down the hallway on her grade 8 graduation as all her teachers and fellow students clap for her(age 13).

Olivia enjoying the wind against her face and hair as she goes for a boat ride with dad at age 14.

Olivia at her local park enjoying the movement on her favourite swing, while humming to her favourite tune - Twinkle Twinkle Little Star at age 14

BEYOND THE PAGES

Writing this book was an incredibly cathartic and healing experience for me. It was an opportunity to share our family's journey through my eyes and leave a lasting legacy for my children. The idea had been brewing within me for quite some time and when the timing felt right, I knew it was meant to be. I wanted my children to understand our challenges and struggles with Olivia and realize that life doesn't always unfold as we expect. It's a journey, not a destination. Through our story, I aim to impart the importance of compassion, resilience, and finding meaning in the face of adversity. Each of our life experiences becomes a chapter in our personal book called "LIFE." Life can be unfair and unjust, but how we choose to interpret and navigate those experiences brings our story to life. When given the chance to share our stories, we are responsible for speaking our truth and showing the world that we are all imperfect humans, doing our best to make the most of our circumstances on this earth.

I believe it is crucial to instill in my children a deep understanding of Olivia's journey, particularly during her early years. I hope that they develop empathy, compassion, and appreciation for embracing individuals who may otherwise be considered "misunderstood" like Olivia. There are countless remarkable individuals with unique perspectives and purposes in life, and my children need to recognize and honour that diversity.

As a parent, I am responsible for teaching them that we are all shaped by our environment and the circumstances we are born into. Life presents us with challenges to navigate and handle, and our response to these challenges defines who we are. I firmly believe in the power of karma and consistently teach my children the value of being compassionate, caring, and generous toward others. By nurturing positive actions and intentions, we create a ripple effect that brings fruitful rewards, such as success, self-worth, personal satisfaction, and love.

I want my children to experience personal growth through self-love and self-respect. I hope they develop a life filled with confidence and resilience, even during the darkest of times amidst the greatest struggles. Most importantly, I wish for them to navigate the world with open hearts, kindness, and a genuine concern for others. By embracing these qualities, they will find inner peace and thrive in the face of today's challenges.

Olivia (14) with her siblings Lauren (7), Chelsea(5) and Julian (16) at Christmas

HEARTFELT TRIBUTE

PERSONAL DEDICATIONS

To my eldest child, Julian,

who bestowed upon me the honoured title of being a mother, I earnestly seek your forgiveness from the depths of my soul. I ask for understanding in the moments when I couldn't be there for you due to the challenges and demands of raising a large, demanding family. I deeply regret the countless baseball games and tournaments I couldn't attend, the missed opportunities to play Legos together or help you build forts in the woods. I am genuinely sorry.

I hope you can understand that throughout those challenging times, my actions were always driven by a mother's unwavering love and dedication to her children. The instinct to protect and provide for you kicked in, and I was in constant fight or flight. Thankfully, your father and extended family supported you every step of the way, showering you with immense love and affection. I know in my heart you were not short of feeling special or like you belonged.

As you now transition into adulthood, I hope you can gain insight into my life's choices. Witnessing the remarkable young man you've become fills my heart with pride and honour. Your tremendous confidence and assertiveness **shine through** your strong and manly physique, and your endless care and compassion for all family members are evident in everything you do. It truly takes a community to raise a family, and I'm grateful for all the surrounding support that has shaped you.

Despite the missed opportunities, I firmly believe that life still holds many moments for us to share and create meaningful experiences together. I eagerly look forward to embracing each of these opportunities with open arms. My love for you knows no boundaries, and I cherish the chance to continue building a strong bond, making up for lost time, and creating beautiful new memories as we journey through life together.

Julian (16) playing for the Ontario Astros at an away tournament with dad

To my little angels, Lauren and Chelsea.

As you read this book one day, I hope you can grasp the immense and heartfelt intention behind my words. Though you may be young now, I trust that as you grow into womanhood and, hopefully, motherhood, you will come to understand why I felt so compelled to write this. You two, my little angels, have been the source of profound inspiration and light in my life, even during the darkest of times. You have helped me see beyond my own challenges and lifted the haze that once enveloped me. You helped me in so many ways than you could ever know. Each day you exist, you bring radiant warmth and endless possibilities into my world.

Your love for Olivia is boundless, and witnessing it has been a gift beyond measure. Growing up in our vibrant and sometimes chaotic family has instilled a sense of confidence, independence, and resilience within each of you. These qualities have been a guiding force in my own journey. My heartfelt prayer is that you both continue to discover your inner purpose and allow your determination and self-belief to transcend any obstacles that may cross your path. With deep conviction, anything and everything is possible.

Know that my love for you knows no bounds. You have brought immeasurable joy into my life, and I am eternally grateful for the privilege of being your mother. Embrace the journey ahead with open hearts and open minds, knowing that I am here to support and love you every step of the way.

Olivia (12) with her sisters Lauren (5) and Chelsea (3)

My dear husband Mark, the words written in this book can never fully express the depth of my gratitude for you and everything you have done and continue to do to make our lifelong journey together filled with comfort, security, and joy. You have surpassed all my expectations in life, being there for me during the most challenging moments when I thought I couldn't bear it alone. Your unwavering support, encouragement, and belief in me have allowed me to confront any hurdle with calm and grace while becoming the absolute best version of me.

Throughout our journey together, we have triumphed over countless challenges, but we have always relied on our shared moral compass, instilled in us from our upbringing, to navigate through those moments and emerge stronger. From relocating our numerous homes to nurturing and raising four incredible children, including one with special needs, we have faced it all as a united front. Whether we are carving through the slopes of Blue Mountain or sailing the pristine waters of Georgian Bay, our world is our oyster to discover. My dearest love and companion of 21 years, you are not just my husband but my closest confidant and ally. I am profoundly grateful for your unwavering presence and steadfast support throughout our earthly journey together. Your strength has been my beacon of light, carrying me through life's darkest tunnels. I hope I can reciprocate, offering you the solace and encouragement you need in return. I eagerly anticipate the years ahead, hand in hand, as we continue to walk through the path we call life.

Dad pointing out the stingrays to Olivia at the Ripleys Acquarium which she found fascinating (age12)

To all of our extended family.

Our family's incredible journey is fueled by the unwavering support of each and every one of you. We couldn't have done it alone. From our cherished sisters, brothers and parents, you have played a vital role in helping us navigate the turbulent waters of raising our children. When we couldn't be there physically, you guided Julian with love and affection. And during the times when Olivia's needs took precedence, your presence brought comfort to our little girls. Together, we have embraced this journey with Olivia, sharing both the burdens and the celebrations. Your love is unconditional and has given us the strength and motivation to keep propelling forward, even when it feels impossible. The thought of facing this lifelong journey alone would have been unbearable, but with your love and support acting as our personal cheerleaders, every step we take gives us hope for a better tomorrow.

Olivia (14) with my parents and Lauren (7)

Olivia turning 12 on her birthday with her dad's parents and her sister Lauren (5)

To all of Olivia's nannies, babysitters, educators, physicians and therapists.

It takes a village to raise these special children, and without each of you, my journey on this earth would be impossible without your guiding light. I am overwhelmed with gratitude for the unwavering guidance and love each of you has poured into Olivia's life. I truly believe, your dedication has shaped her into the joyful, thriving soul she is today.

Your commitment to Olivia's well-being shines as a beacon of boundless love in the face of adversity. Your belief in her potential fuels every step she takes forward and every milestone she achieves, even when no one sees it. You are the reason that light shines within Olivia. Mrs. Morton, Mrs. Butlin, the compassionate staff at St. Nicholas and St. Mike's, and the extraordinary souls like Aaliya, Julia, Maria, and Noemia are more than mere helpers—they are guardian angels hand-picked by the good Lord above to walk alongside Olivia. Your impact goes beyond measure, reminding us of the profound influence each person can have on another's life. May God's blessings continue to shower upon you, lighting your path as you touch the lives of those around you with grace, compassion, and boundless love.

I will take this opportunity to also extend heartfelt gratitude on behalf of all the families touched by these special children. Your presence and dedication mean the world to us. You are making an immeasurable difference; we are forever thankful for that.

Olivia's with Mrs. Morton, her special education teacher at Palgrave school (age 4)

Olivia with Mrs.Butlin, her special education teacher at Macville School (age 8)

Olivia at her grade 8 graduation with Mrs. C & Mrs. Gennara at St. Nicholas School (age 13)

Olivia and her schoolmate Michael with their highschool teachers from St. Michaels Secondary School on a school trip (age 16)

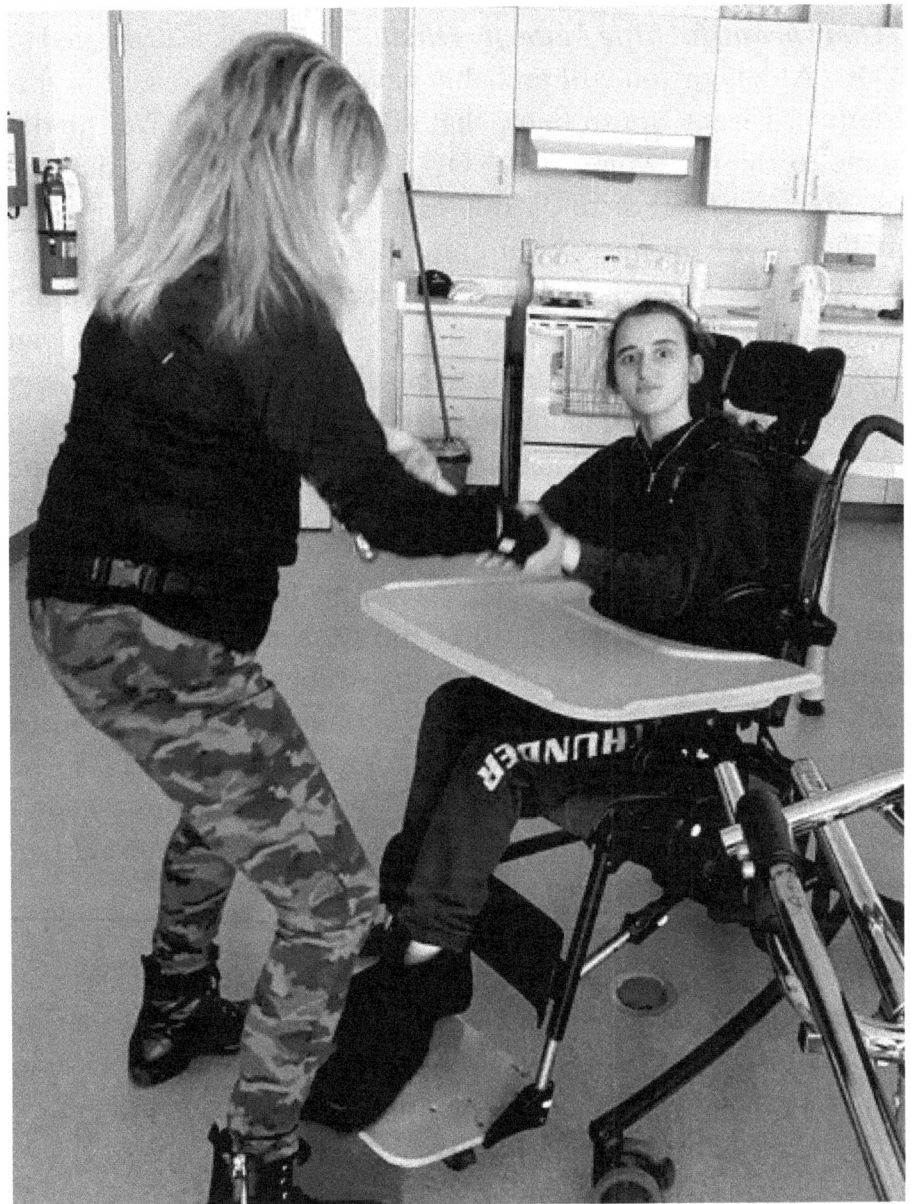

*Olivia dancing with Mrs. Codeiro at
St. Michaels Secondary School (age 17)*

TO my beautiful little butterfly Olivia. This book is dedicated to YOU. Although you will probably never be able to read it in this lifetime, I want you to know that after 17 years, I have finally come to the realization that YOU are one of my life's purposes. Your existence here on this earth being sent to me as your mother, is ***my purpose***. I am grateful for the invaluable lessons you've imparted – patience, resilience, acceptance, and inner confidence. Through your guidance, I've learned that life can persist even in the face of unbearable challenges, revealing silver linings in every dark moment. Your sheer existence has shown me the importance of rising above difficulties and embracing the broader perspective.

Every day, I offer prayers and extend birthday wishes, hoping that you continue living the best life possible during our time together. As your earthly mother, my deepest desire is for your siblings to perpetuate their love and compassion for you in the coming years. My sincere wish is for your next journey to be free from seizures and mental haze. To rise from the shadows that once enveloped your earthly existence. To awaken into an entirely new world. A whole new dimension.

I envision you gracefully transitioning into a new life, shining through much like a peaceful colorful monarch butterfly soaring freely in the clear blue skies. May you look down upon a world that was once filled with limitations, now transformed into a realm of boundless possibilities.

Olivia (age 14) giving me a deep stare as her eyes always tell a story

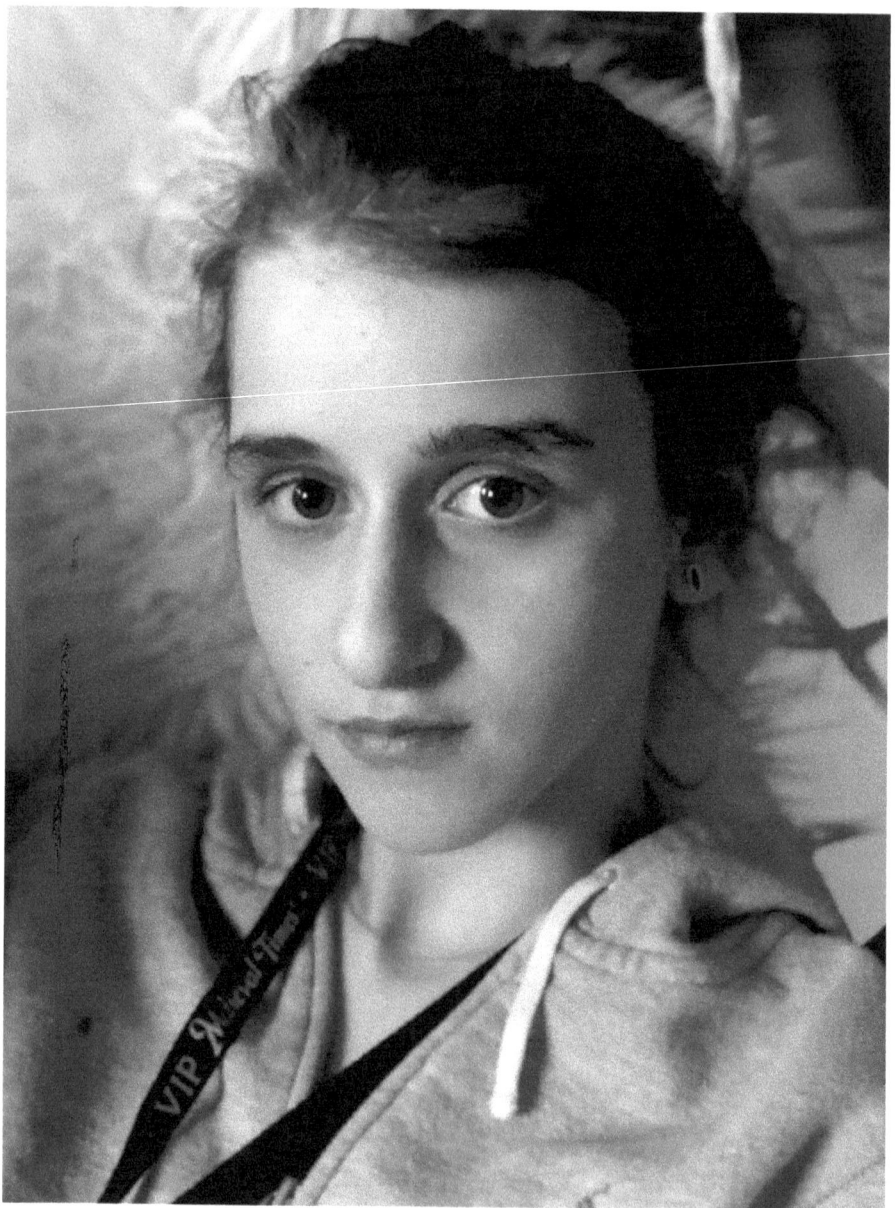
Olivia (age 15) on her bedroom swing enjoying the movement

This book is dedicated to you, my cherished readers.

I would like to start with immense gratitude for those who took a leap of faith and delved into the narrative of our family's journey. The decision to explore our experiences together means more to me than words can convey.

I sincerely hope this story kindles a flame of inspiration within you, providing the strength and determination to persevere even in the darkest moments. Every day, remarkable souls like Olivia come into existence, and as parents navigate the complexities of purpose and existence, I aim for this book to serve as a poignant reminder. With all its hurdles and challenges, life continues to shape itself, unfolding in ways that affirm our resilience and capacity for growth.

Within every difficulty and impossibility, glimmers of hope and hidden gems are waiting to be discovered. By holding onto hope in our hearts and surrounding ourselves with a supportive network, we have the power to conquer any obstacle and bravely place one foot in front of the other and propel forward. Even in our darkest days, it is essential to focus on what brings us immense joy and to remember that tomorrow brings with it a new dawn—a day filled with renewed hope, opportunities, and endless possibilities.

May this book serve as a guiding light, reminding you that you are never alone in your journey. Together, we can overcome adversity and find solace in the knowledge that a brighter tomorrow is always waiting for us. Keep moving forward, my dear readers, and let your hearts be filled with unwavering hope, with warmth and understanding, Liana Cancian.

Olivia (8) with her extended family on her dads side during Christmas

Olivia (11) celebrating her Uncle Nico's birthday, along with all of her cousins

Olivia (12) with her sisters Chelsea (3) and Lauren (5) on Halloween

Olivia (9) with her family at a wedding

*Olivia (11) with her family posing for a
Christmas card on their country property*

Myself and Olivia (age 11)

Olivia (12) going for a hike with her family on Easter day

Olivia with her family celebrating her Sweet 16

ABOUT THE AUTHOR

Liana Cancian's journey unfolds in a quaint city just outside of Toronto, where she was raised by immigrant parents who instilled in her the virtues of resilience and compassion. Graduating with a degree from the University of Toronto, she initially pursued a thriving career in pharmaceutical sales. However, her life took a profound turn when she embraced her true calling as a devoted wife and mother to four children, one of whom required special care.

The turning point came with the diagnosis of her special needs child, redirecting Liana's life purpose. From that point forward, she devoted herself tirelessly to advocating for her daughter's well-being while juggling the demands of a bustling household. Her story, a blend of perseverance and hope, resonates deeply and is shared on various podcasts and within special needs communities, offering glimpses of both adversity and inspiration.

Despite encountering life's challenges, Liana finds solace in actively engaging with her community. Whether she's delivering meals to seniors, organizing charitable events, or nurturing her own well-being through activities like yoga and indulging in a newfound passion for pickleball with friends, her commitment to making a positive impact knows no bounds. With her book ready to shed light on new pathways and potentially open doors to a podcast that echoes her message of resilience, Liana endeavours to inspire others through her journey of discovering hope in the face of darkness.

Her ultimate aspiration is to leave behind a lasting legacy for her children and future generations to cherish.

With warmth and understanding,
Liana Cancian
416-726-8473
lianacancian@live.ca

ABOUT THE PUBLISHER

Dear Reader,

As you hold this remarkable book in your hands, we want to express our heartfelt gratitude for becoming a part of the Live Life Happy Community of readers. Your curiosity and thirst for knowledge fuel our passion for publishing meaningful non-fiction works.

At Live Life Happy Publishing, our mission is rooted in bringing forth literature that not only entertains but uplifts, supports, and nourishes the soul. We firmly believe that books have the power to transform lives, to ignite passions, and to spread joy far and wide.

Behind every word, every chapter, lies the dedication of our authors who pour their hearts and souls into their craft. Their ultimate aim? To touch your life in profound ways, to inspire, and to leave an indelible mark on your journey.

Your role in this journey is invaluable; by sharing your thoughts through reviews, spreading the word to others, or reaching out to the authors themselves, you become an integral part of sparking transformation in countless lives, igniting a ripple effect of joy and enlightenment.

And if, perchance, you or someone you know has dreams of writing, of sharing a message, or of unleashing a powerful story unto the world, know that Live Life Happy Publishing stands ready to guide you. Our doors are open, our ears attuned, and our hearts eager to hear your tale.

So, dear reader, let us, continue to spread the magic of literature, one page at a time. Reach out, share, and most importantly, never underestimate the power of your message to touch lives.

With warmest regards,

LiveLifeHappyPublishing.com

P.S. Remember, books change lives. Whose life will you touch with yours?

www.ingramcontent.com/pod-product-compliance
Lightning Source LLC
Chambersburg PA
CBHW060655100426
42734CB00047B/1884